THE WORLD WAR II EXPERIENCE

AN INTERACTIVE HISTORY ADVENTURE

CAPSTONE PRESS
a capstone imprint

Edge Books are published by Capstone Press,
1710 Roe Crest Drive, North Mankato, Minnesota 56003
www.capstonepub.com

Library of Congress Cataloging-in-Publication Data
Cataloging-in-publication information is on file with the Library of Congress.
ISBN 978-1-4914-1711-9 (paper over board)
ISBN 978-1-4765-2169-5 (paperback)

Photo Credits
AP Images, 8, 147, 188, 206, Henry L. Griffin, 214, U.S. Signal Corps, 213; Corbis, 232, 290, Bettmann, 230, 307, 315, Hulton-Deutsch Collection, 269; Courtesy of the National Park Service, USS Arizona Memorial, 41, 58, 80, 94; The Franklin D. Roosevelt Library, 248, 257, 301, 320; Getty Images, Inc: AFP, 142, Hulton Archive, 196, Keystone, 17, 21, 125, 162, MPI, 102, 195, 210, Popperfoto, 161, Popperfoto/Paul Popper, 183, Time Life Pictures/John Florea, 208, J.R. Eyerman, 96, Dmitri Kessel, 176, Mansell, 116, William C. Shrout, 181, William Vandivert, 168, Time Life Pictures/Timepix/Hugo Jaeger, 120, 137; Library of Congress: Prints and Photographs Division, 67, 88, 150, 241, 266, 282, 285, 293, 317, 319; Maxwell Air Force Base, Alabama, 305; National Archives and Record Administration (NARA), 165, 224, 227, 237, 239, 245, 251, 253, 277, 286, 310, 322, U.S. Army, 156, Boyle, 184, U.S. Marine Corps/Pvt. Bob Bailey, cover (middle), U.S. Navy, cover (bottom), 26, 30, 45, 86, 228, CPhoM. H.S. Fawcett, 101, 264, U.S. Sgt. Thomas D. Barnett, 203; National WASP WWII Museum, Sweetwater, Texas, 261; Shutterstock: Ivan Cholakov, cover (top), Robert Adrian Hillman, design element; United States Holocaust Memorial Museum, Bep Meyer Zion (The views expressed in this book and the context in which the image is used do not necessarily reflect the views or policy of, nor imply approval or endorsement by, the USHMM), 131; United States Navy: PH3 (AW/SW) Jayme Pastoric, 106; U.S. Naval Historical Center, 12, 15, 19, 34, 42, 48, 50, 56, 64, 71, 77, 91, photo by Warrant Officer Obie Newcomb, Jr. (USMCR), 192; Zuma Press: Contra Costa Times/Photo courtesy Benjamin Smith, 98

Printed in the United States of America in Chicago, Illinois.
022014 008022

Table of Contents

The Attack on Pearl Harbor:

An Interactive History Adventure

By Allison Lassieur

Consultant:
David Aiken
Codirector, Pearl Harbor History Associates
Stratford, Connecticut

Table of Contents

About Your Adventure

YOU are living in the early 1940s. Much of the world is at war. The United States hopes to stay out of it. But Americans keep a close eye on events in Europe and Japan. When efforts to keep the peace fail, whose side will you choose?

In this book, you'll explore how the choices people made meant the difference between life and death. The events you'll experience happened to real people.

Chapter One sets the scene. Then you choose which path to read. Follow the directions at the bottom of each page. The choices you make will change your outcome. After you finish one path, go back and read the others for new perspectives and more adventures.

YOU CHOOSE the path you take through history.

Leaders from Japan, Italy, and Germany signed an agreement to help each other in war.

CHAPTER 1

A World at War

It is November 1941, and the world is at war. The fighting started in the 1930s, as powerful leaders dreamed of expanding their empires. Now, the leaders of Japan, Italy, and Germany have signed an agreement to help each other reach their goals. Together, these countries are called the Axis powers.

Most of the world is focused on fighting in Europe. In 1939, German ruler Adolf Hitler invaded Poland. Since then, Denmark, Norway, Luxembourg, and France have fallen to Germany.

Turn the page.

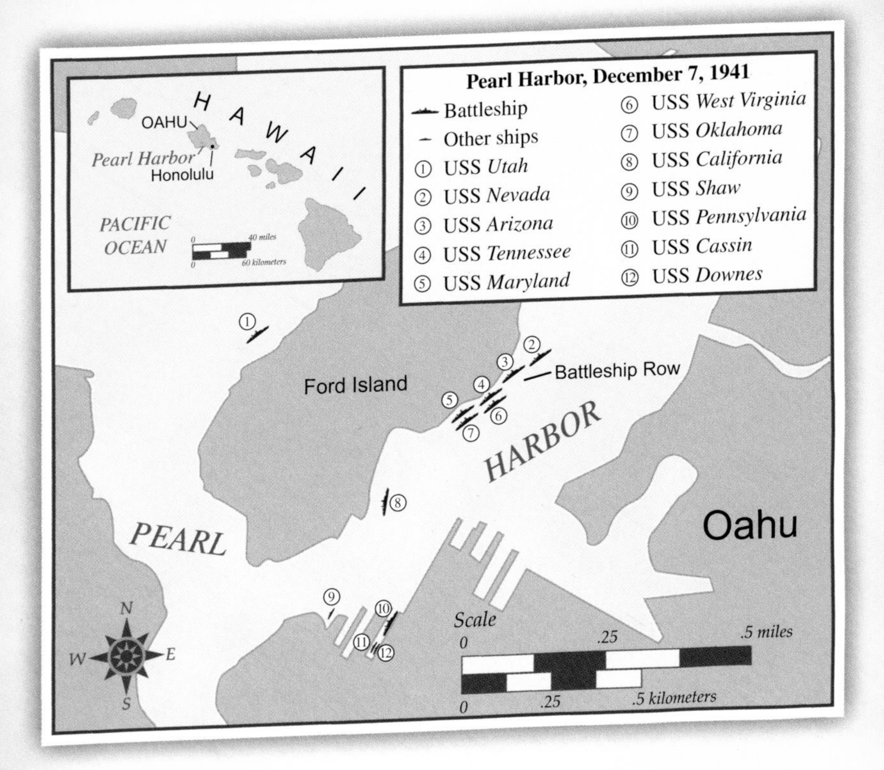

But before there was war in Europe, there was war in Asia. In Japan, military leaders want more land and more natural resources. In 1931, they took control of the Chinese region of Manchuria. In 1937, they attacked China. Now they occupy most of eastern China. Japanese leaders talk of bringing all of Asia under their control.

Meanwhile, the United States hopes to avoid fighting. Instead of soldiers, U.S. President Franklin D. Roosevelt sends money to Great Britain. He cuts off trade with Japan.

By early December 1941, the situation is desperate. War is coming. You just don't know when or where.

Then, on the morning of December 7, 1941, something happens that will change the course of the war. And you find yourself right in the middle of it.

To be a Japanese pilot, turn to page 13.

To be a U.S. Navy sailor, turn to page 51.

To be a U.S. Navy nurse stationed at the Pearl Harbor naval base, turn to page 81.

Admiral Isoroku Yamamoto planned the surprise attack on Pearl Harbor.

CHAPTER 2

Master of the Attack

As an officer in the Japanese Navy, you are one of the few who know about a top secret plan. For a few years, Admiral Isoroku Yamamoto and other leaders have been planning to attack the United States.

Yamamoto believes that only the United States has the power to stop Japan's expansion. But Japan lacks the resources to win a long, drawn-out war with America. A sudden, swift attack could destroy the U.S. naval fleet. While it recovered, America would be unable to join the war. Meanwhile, Japan could expand as it wants.

Turn the page.

Yamamoto's plan must be kept secret, even from your fellow pilots. If any hint of the attack gets out, the mission will fail.

In the late summer of 1941, you and your fellow pilots begin training. Fighter pilots practice air combat. Bomber pilots learn attack formations and how to drop torpedoes from very low levels. The torpedo planes fly so low that they almost touch the rooftops of nearby houses. The commanding officers study maps and models of Pearl Harbor and Oahu Island, where the United States keeps its fleet.

Under the cover of darkness on November 26, 1941, the attack fleet slips out of Tokyo Harbor. There are six aircraft carriers, *Akagi, Hiryu, Kaga, Shokaku, Soryu,* and *Zuikaku.* The fleet also includes battleships, cruisers, submarines, destroyers, and more than 400 airplanes. It is the largest strike force you've ever seen.

The Japanese aircraft carrier *Zuikaku* was part of the attack force headed to Pearl Harbor.

You are aboard the aircraft carrier *Akagi*. The strike force heads for the launch point 200 miles north of Oahu. In early December, Vice Admiral Chuichi Nagumo gathers everyone together. "I can now tell you what your mission is," he says. "We are on our way to Pearl Harbor in Hawaii. We will attack the American military base there. You are to destroy every battleship and aircraft carrier there."

Turn the page.

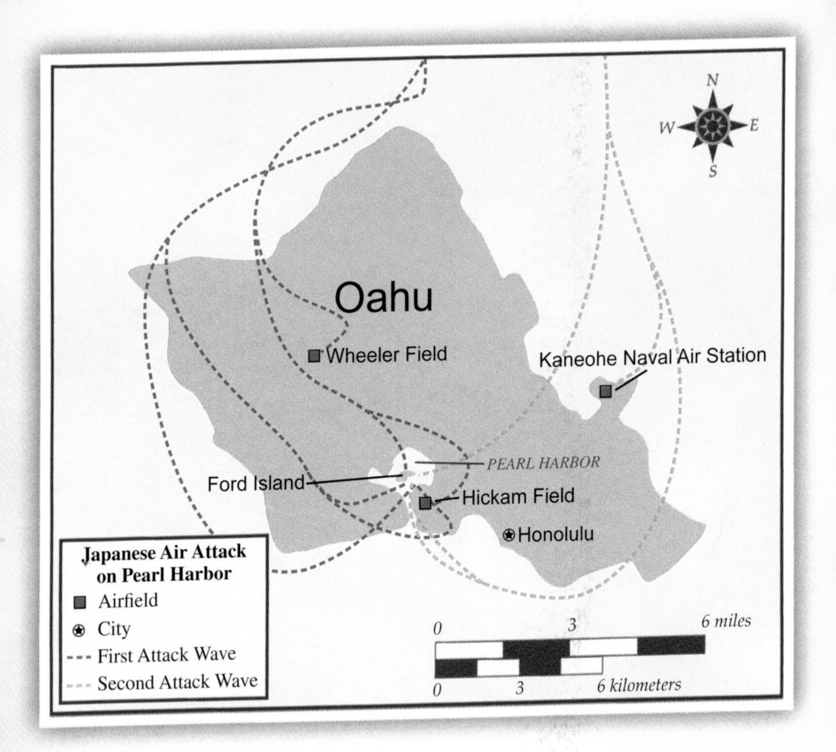

Everyone starts talking at once. Nagumo quiets the crowd. "The attack will happen in two waves. The first group will attack the battleships and carriers. The second wave will attack what is left. Meanwhile, small submarines called midget subs will sneak into the harbor. We will attack the Americans from every side."

Japanese pilots received their orders before taking off from the aircraft carrier.

You're sure the attack will be a great moment for Japan. The world will finally understand your country's power. No matter what role you play in the attack, you will be making history.

To join the first wave of the attack, turn to page **18**.

To join the second wave of pilots, turn to page **23**.

The attack will begin at 6:00 in the morning on December 7. The night before, nobody sleeps. You talk for hours with the other pilots. Most of you are hopeful and proud of Japan for this bold attack. But some of the pilots are nervous. They say the sneak attack goes against the ancient Japanese customs of Samurai warriors. "The Samurai used to say, 'It does not do to slit the throat of a sleeping man,'" one pilot says. "It is wrong to attack without warning."

The next morning before you board your plane, you tie a white cloth called a *hachimaki* around your forehead. The cloth is marked with the symbol of the Rising Sun, just like on the Japanese flag. Written on the cloth are the Japanese words for "sure victory." Wearing the cloth means you are ready to die for your country.

Japanese planes wait to take off from an aircraft carrier the morning of December 7, 1941.

As you wait for your turn to take off, the ship pitches and rolls. You must wait for the winds to die down. Fifteen minutes later, you finally take off into the darkness.

Turn the page.

Your plane and more than 180 others roar south toward Pearl Harbor. As dawn spills over the horizon, all you see is the ocean below. Sunbeams shine through the clouds like the red beams on the Japanese Navy's flag.

When the clouds disappear, it becomes a beautiful, clear morning. You can see for miles. Finally, you glimpse land. Hawaii! It is a glorious sight. And there are no American fighters to greet you. Your attack force has surprised the Americans.

Commander Mitsuo Fuchida led the air attack on Pearl Harbor.

At 7:40, Commander Mitsuo Fuchida shoots a black flare. It is the signal to change into the attack formation. Nine minutes later, you hear a signal tapped over your radio. "*To, to, to,*" it says. Attack! The first planes begin dropping bombs on Wheeler Field. This fighter base is in the middle of the island of Oahu.

Turn the page.

At 7:51, you hear the signal "*To-ra, To-ra, To-ra.*" This signal tells you that the Americans have been taken by surprise.

By now, you're close enough to clearly see buildings, hangars, and other structures. A few pilots break away and head toward Hickam Field. Other pilots continue on to the harbor. Which direction do you go?

To head toward Hickam Field, turn to page 25.

To continue to the harbor, turn to page 26.

The first wave flies into the darkness, and the waiting begins. The ship is oddly quiet. Feeling restless, you make your way to the railing of the deck. There, you see a signal flag snapping in the wind. "The fate of the Empire rests on this battle. Let everyone do his duty," it says.

All around you, the planes are being readied for the takeoff of the second wave. You go to your plane and test the controls.

Finally, the carriers turn into the wind. At 7:15, your commander, Shigekazu Shimazaki, gives the order to take off. One by one, the 167 planes rise into the sky. You circle into formation and head south.

Turn the page.

At 7:49, you receive the radio signal telling you that the first wave has just begun its attack. A few minutes later, you get a second radio signal. It tells you the surprise attack was successful.

At about 8:45, you notice a low, dark cloud over the ocean. It is the smoke over Pearl Harbor. You move into attack formation. Some pilots head toward the harbor. Others are going to attack the airfields. If the planes are not destroyed, American pilots could fight back.

To fly to the harbor, turn to page 39.

To attack the airfields, turn to page 44.

You fly to Hickam Field on the southern edge of the harbor. Airplanes are lined up in neat rows. Perfect targets! This is going to be easier than you expected.

You fly low over the line of airplanes, looking for a good target. Planes ahead of you are dropping their bombs. Suddenly, an explosion clouds the air with black smoke. You can't see anything on the ground except smoke and fire. You are pretty sure you're close to a target. You could keep going and hope your bomb hits. But you don't want to waste your only bomb. Maybe you should circle around again. You have a split second to decide.

To pull out of your dive, turn to page **29**.

To keep diving, turn to page **31**.

American battleships were docked side by side in two neat rows.

You head for the harbor. As you approach, you see that your main targets, the carriers, are not there. Disappointed, you look for the battleships. They sit in two neat rows, completely undefended. You fly high in the sky and continue on toward the huge navy fleet.

To attack USS Arizona, *go to page* 27.

To attack USS Tennessee, *turn to page* 34.

You join the formation of planes heading toward *Arizona*. The battleship sits along the edge of Ford Island. On the deck, American sailors are gathered to raise the flag. They look confused as planes scream overhead. As bombs begin to fall, they scatter quickly. Soon it is your turn. You lock the target ship in your bombsight.

Before you can drop your bomb, an explosion in the front half of *Arizona* shakes the air. Flames cover the ship. A cloud of dark red smoke shoots up to the height of your plane. Tiny pieces of metal hit the planes ahead of you. In only a few seconds, *Arizona* is destroyed.

You still have a bomb to drop. You circle around again with your formation. As a group, you head toward *Nevada*, just beyond *Arizona*.

Turn the page.

Arizona's thick smoke makes your target hard to see. You can't tell if you're too close. If you don't drop your bomb at just the right time, you could miss. You don't want to waste your only bomb. Should you drop the bomb, or should you circle around again?

To make another pass, turn to page 32.

To drop the bomb, turn to page 33.

"Live now to fight later," you think, quickly pulling out of the dive. It's a good thing you did. Below, debris and smoke swirl in the air.

You climb safely higher and circle the airfield again. It's still hard to see through the smoke and flames. After three passes, you finally spot a few airplanes on the ground. You dive toward them.

"It's a clear shot," you think as you drop your bomb. The blast rips through the airfield as planes shatter into twisted metal. Gasoline from the engines catches fire, causing more explosions. American soldiers scurry below you, dodging flying metal and trying to put out the fires.

Turn the page.

Bombers destroyed airplanes on the ground at Pearl Harbor.

A signal comes over your radio announcing that the first attack is complete. You are to return to the carrier at once. As you climb into the air, you look at the destruction below. Dozens of fires rage out of control. Black smoke chokes the air. Admiral Yamamoto will be very pleased.

THE END

To follow another path, turn to page 11.
To read the conclusion, turn to page 103.

Circling around would give the Americans time to fire back. You must keep going. With a shout, you fly your plane straight into the cloud of smoke. Suddenly, your airplane shudders violently. You've been hit by something. The plane shakes again. You struggle with the controls.

Frantically, you look for somewhere to land. There's so much black smoke that you can't see the ground. Your plane goes into a steep dive. There's nothing you can do now. You're going to crash.

It is dishonorable to be captured. Instead, you decide to use your plane as a weapon. You're strangely calm as you guide your plane straight toward a group of buildings on the ground.

THE END

To follow another path, turn to page 11.
To read the conclusion, turn to page 103.

You'd rather be certain than sorry. You circle around once, then twice. On your third pass, you finally drop your bomb.

As you fly away, you look back to see whether your bomb hit. Instead of smoke and flames, all you see are ripples on the water. Your bomb missed. You curse your bad luck at wasting your only bomb.

At that moment, a signal comes over your radio to return to the carriers. There's nothing more you can do here. You turn your plane toward the open sea and fly back to the aircraft carrier. You're not looking forward to reporting your miss, but you're happy that the attack was successful.

THE END

To follow another path, turn to page 11.
To read the conclusion, turn to page 103.

You decide to take your chances. You drop the bomb and look to see if it hit the target. You see slight damage to *Nevada*. Your bomb hit, but it wasn't accurate enough to cause serious damage. You should have waited.

A signal comes over your radio to return to base. You fly high into the sky and follow the rest of the planes back to the carrier.

Turn to page **48.**

You search the harbor for *Tennessee.* Then you see it, wedged between the shore and another ship, USS *West Virginia.* There's nowhere *Tennessee* can go.

West Virginia was struck by up to nine torpedoes during the attack.

Boom! You hear several explosions, and you fly around to get a better look. *West Virginia* and *Tennessee* are on fire. American sailors on the deck of *Tennessee* spray the flames with hoses.

Suddenly, something hits your plane. That's when you see several antiaircraft guns on *Tennessee* pointed at you. More bullets whiz past your plane.

To keep attacking Tennessee, *turn to page* **36**.

To fly away, turn to page **37**.

No American antiaircraft fire is going to stop you from your mission! You grit your teeth and make another run, dropping your bomb as you pass over *Tennessee*. You see it hit one of the turrets on the ship, but you can't tell if it exploded. Cursing, you circle your plane to get a better look.

Suddenly, your plane rocks violently. You've been hit! Those American gunners are better than you expected. They've shot right through your engine. Smoke billows from your airplane as it falls faster and faster toward the water. As your plane splashes violently into the water, you become one of the few Japanese casualties of the attack.

THE END

To follow another path, turn to page 11.
To read the conclusion, turn to page 103.

You didn't expect antiaircraft fire, and you don't want to be caught in it. You pull your plane higher, out of range of the American guns.

When you're above *Tennessee*, you drop your bomb. It somehow misses its target. The bomb falls into the water, exploding harmlessly.

Turn the page.

At that moment, you hear the signal to return to the carrier. You climb into the sky and look at the destruction below. You can't believe what you see. It looks as if all of the battleships are either destroyed or badly damaged. There is so much black smoke in the sky that you have trouble seeing. Flames cover many of the ships and Ford Island beyond.

"Returning to base," you reply. You're looking forward to reporting to Vice Admiral Nagumo. The attack was a bigger success than you ever imagined.

THE END

To follow another path, turn to page 11.
To read the conclusion, turn to page 103.

As you reach the harbor, you can make out a line of battleships along Ford Island. Smoke pours from some. Others spout waves of oil from their sides. You begin a steep dive toward the ships.

You catch USS *Pennsylvania* in your sight. But from the corner of your eye, you see USS *Nevada* moving slowly toward the channel out of Pearl Harbor. What luck! If you could sink *Nevada,* it would block the channel. No ships would be able to escape. You must decide quickly.

To go after Nevada, *turn to page* **40**.

To continue attacking Pennsylvania, *turn to page* **42**.

It is more important to block the harbor. You pull out of your dive. You and several other bombers swarm like bees above *Nevada*.

You swoop down again and release your bomb. At the same time, you pull back on the control stick. As you zoom upward, several bombs hit the ship. You hope that one of them was yours.

There's nothing more you can do. You soar overhead and watch other bombers go after the ship. After a few minutes, the ship turns slightly. It ends up on shore along the side of the channel. You didn't block the channel, but at least you damaged the ship.

You look at the harbor. Smoke and flames fill the air. There are piles of smoking, twisted metal where buildings and airplanes used to be. Several battleships are on fire, and a few were sunk.

Smoke poured from burning ships while *Oklahoma* slowly sank.

As you fly back to the carrier, a strange combination of pride and fear overcomes you. You are very proud that Japan was so successful. But you worry that the Americans will soon be waging war on Japan. There is no way to know what will happen then.

THE END

To follow another path, turn to page 11.
To read the conclusion, turn to page 103.

While other bombers go after *Nevada,* you continue your dive toward *Pennsylvania.* You fly nearer and nearer until the target nearly fills your sight. Just then, the ship bursts into flames. Another pilot has scored a direct hit.

Only one bomb hit *Pennsylvania.* It returned to service after just a few months.

As you look for a new target, a message comes through your radio. The attack is almost complete. All pilots should prepare to return to the carriers. But you still have a bomb, and you don't want to waste it. Maybe you could find another ship to attack. What do you do next?

To head toward another ship, turn to page 45.

To return to the carrier, turn to page 48.

You head toward Kaneohe Naval Air Station. There isn't much left. Below you, shattered planes and buildings cover the ground. Black smoke fills the air.

Suddenly, something hits your plane. Gunfire! To your astonishment, you see several American planes roaring toward you.

"Where did they come from?" you mutter as you frantically dodge and dive to avoid the gunfire. The planes must have survived the first attack. Several of your fellow pilots are shot down around you. For the first time, you wonder if you're going to survive the day. A U.S. plane speeds toward you, its guns blazing.

To shoot back, turn to page **46**.

To try to get away, turn to page **47**.

Fire caused the ammunition on *Shaw* to explode.

You head toward USS *Shaw*. It is docked near *Pennsylvania*. Several bombs have already hit *Shaw*, and it is burning. You dive toward the ship and drop your bomb. A massive blast rips through the ship. A huge ball of fire shoots into the air toward your plane. You watch as the entire ship and dock are swallowed in flames and smoke.

Turn to page 47.

You're not going to run! With a yell, you fire at the American plane. But you're not fast enough. Bullets rip through the cockpit, hitting you in several places. You scream in pain and let go of the controls as the cockpit fills with smoke. "This is it," you tell yourself. At least you were part of the successful attack. Japan will be proud of you, even if you don't make it back home.

THE END

To follow another path, turn to page 11.
To read the conclusion, turn to page 103.

As you quickly pull your plane out of danger, you receive the signal to return to the carriers. You and several other pilots head back to the aircraft carriers.

As you fly away, you take one last look at Pearl Harbor. Although a few ships still float in the harbor, most of them are badly damaged. The airfields on the island are almost destroyed. Many buildings, including machine shops, ammunition buildings, and storage buildings, are flattened. It will take months, maybe years, for the U.S. Navy to recover.

Turn the page.

You arrive safely back on your ship, tired but happy. You and the other pilots report on the attack. All of the pilots, including you, are eager to return for a third attack. Perhaps you could find the U.S. aircraft carriers.

Vice Admiral Nagumo is disturbed that there were no aircraft carriers at Pearl Harbor. He is worried that the U.S. carriers will find the Japanese attack force.

Vice Admiral Chuichi Nagumo was in charge of the attack force against Pearl Harbor.

Finally, Nagumo makes a decision. "There will be no more attacks," he says.

You can't believe it. You stare in amazement as Nagumo continues.

"It is too dangerous," Nagumo says. "We have achieved success here. We took the Americans by surprise and destroyed their navy. Our mission is complete, and it is time to return to Japan."

When you and the rest of the attack force arrive in Tokyo, you are welcomed as heroes for your bravery. That makes you happy. But the Americans have declared war on Japan. You'll be seeing them in battle again.

To follow another path, turn to page 11.
To read the conclusion, turn to page 103.

Arizona served in the Pacific during the 1930s and came to Pearl Harbor in 1940.

CHAPTER 3

Caught by Surprise

It is late 1941, and you are a young navy sailor, fresh from basic training. You're ready to serve your country, but you're nervous. Every day, you hear frightening rumors. Some people say Adolf Hitler will invade the United States. Others say that could never happen. Everyone is restless and uneasy. You don't know how long the United States can stay out of the war.

You are assigned to *Arizona* in Pearl Harbor. An assignment in Hawaii is a dream job, and you feel lucky. The weather is always mild. When you're not on duty, you and your friends spend time outdoors. You hike in the lush forests of Oahu or swim in the clear blue ocean.

Turn the page.

You live on the battleship in a room below the deck with several other sailors. You wake up early on Sunday, December 7. Sunday is your day to relax. You don't have any duties, so you and some of your buddies have requested shore leave this morning. They want to spend the day on the beach, and it sounds like fun. But you are feeling a bit lazy. Staying on board and relaxing also seems like a good idea.

To get up and join your friends, go to page 53.

To stay in your room and relax, turn to page 55.

If you're going to go ashore, you'd better get up now and get some breakfast. You dress quickly and make your way to the mess hall. It's not too crowded, and you easily find your friends.

"Looks like another gorgeous Sunday," you say as you sit down.

"You bet," your friend Bob answers, his mouth full of food. "Just think, a whole day off!"

While you discuss your plans for the day, another sailor sits down with you. "Hey, did you guys hear about the submarine they saw near the harbor?" he says.

"You mean an enemy sub?" you ask.

"Yeah, Japanese, I think," the sailor replies.

Turn the page.

"Oh, I don't believe it," your friend Tom says. "There's no way a Japanese sub could get here. The harbor is crawling with navy ships!"

After breakfast, you and your buddies go to the upper deck to watch the flag-raising ceremony. In the distance, you see a large group of airplanes flying toward the harbor.

"Who is that?" you ask.

"It's probably the bomber pilots that are supposed to come back today," Bob replies.

"Those guys are flying really low," Tom says.

Suddenly, an explosion rocks the ship. You don't know what's going on or what to do next.

To run to find an officer, turn to page **56**.

To run to the railing to see what happened, turn to page **58**.

Maybe you'll go to shore later, but for now, you decide to stay in your room. Your roommates are already gone. It's quiet for once, and you're going to enjoy it while you can. You prop yourself up and grab a book.

After a while, you hear the navy band playing "Stars and Stripes" on the deck above you. It must be about 8:00, time to raise the flag. You decide to get dressed.

Suddenly, the ship shudders. You hear a thud and shouts from the upper decks. You rush into the hallway. A sailor runs past, shouting, "We're under attack!"

You have no idea what to do. Your commanding officer is nowhere to be seen.

To try to find an officer to get orders, turn to page 56.

To go to your battle station, turn to page 66.

You and several others run toward the officers' quarters, hoping for news. Black smoke fills the air. The smell of burning oil and metal stings your nose.

You see Rear Admiral Isaac Kidd, the commander, running toward you. "Get to your battle stations!" he shouts. "Japan has attacked! This is not a drill!" Then he heads for the signal bridge.

Rear Admiral Isaac C. Kidd became the commander of *Arizona* in 1938.

Bombs rain down from above. You race to the ammunition storage area. It's your job to make sure the guns have enough ammunition to return fire. As you turn a corner, you nearly trip over a sailor lying on the floor. He's out cold.

You need to get to your battle station fast. But you want to help the injured sailor.

To continue to your battle station, turn to page **66**.

To try to help the injured sailor, turn to page **67**.

When you get to the railing, all you see is the airplanes filling the sky. Each plane is marked with a red circle. It's the Japanese symbol of the Rising Sun. Meatballs, you and your buddies call the symbols. You never thought you'd see Japanese planes flying over Pearl Harbor.

The Rising Sun is a symbol of Japan. The symbol was painted on Japanese planes.

People run and yell as the Japanese planes whiz past. Then another explosion rocks the ship. You grab hold of the railing to keep from being thrown overboard. Several men flip over the railing, screaming as they fall. At that moment, you hear a voice over the loudspeaker shout, "To your battle stations! This is not a drill!" You start to run to your battle station below the deck. But then you hear cries for help coming from the sailors in the water.

If you stay to help the sailors who fell overboard, turn to page **60**.

If you obey orders and head to your battle station, turn to page **66**.

You have to try to help these guys in the water. You haul a rope to the railing and throw it to the nearest man.

"Grab it!" you shout. With all your strength, you pull the man from the water. "Thanks," he gasps. He claps you on the back and runs off.

You wish you could help the others, but they're too far away. You climb down the nearest hatch and run through the passageway. You join a group of sailors running in the same direction. Suddenly, the ship shakes. The lights go out.

When the emergency lights flicker on, you see water rushing toward you. "Quick, open that other hatch," you say.

"It's jammed," another man answers. The water is rising fast. What do you do?

To go back the way you came, go to page **61**.

To try opening the hatch, turn to page **62**.

"Follow me!" You lead the men back down the way you came. The water is up to your waist now, and it's getting hard to walk.

Suddenly, the ship shakes violently. You hear several thuds from above you, and then a loud hissing noise. A rush of hot wind blows past your face. A ball of flame roars down the passageway. It's the last thing you'll ever see. You and hundreds of other young men burn to death aboard *Arizona*.

THE END

To follow another path, turn to page 11.
To read the conclusion, turn to page 103.

Another man, an officer, quiets the group. "If we can loosen the latches, we can get out of here," he says. "There's one set at the top of the hatch and one set at the bottom."

With a deep breath, you dive into the waist-deep water. You feel your way around the hatch until you find the latches. You pull several times, and they move a little. You come up for air.

"I've almost got them," you say. You dive again and pull. The latches give way! You come up again and shout to everyone, "Open the hatch before the water pressure is too high!"

Seven pairs of hands pull the hatch open. Water drains into the hatch as you and the other men climb through the hatch to safety.

On deck, bodies lie everywhere. Smoke chokes the air. The ship leans so far to one side that you can hardly believe that it hasn't sunk. Several men abandon the ship, jumping into the water. But if you stay on board, you might be able to save other sailors. What do you do next?

To abandon the ship, turn to page **64**.

To stay on board, turn to page **65**.

The wreckage of USS *Arizona* burned for several days after the attack.

"We've got to abandon ship," you shout. You and the other men quickly drop a lifeboat into the water and climb into it. As you paddle away, a huge explosion seems to blow open the sky. *Arizona* is lost in flames and black smoke. In just a few minutes, the ship sinks.

You've survived the sinking of *Arizona*. All you can do now is wait for a rescue boat.

THE END

To follow another path, turn to page 11.
To read the conclusion, turn to page 103.

"I'm going to stay here and help these guys," you say to the others. You start checking the bodies for signs of life. Most of the men are badly burned. Some of them have deep cuts from metal debris. None of them are alive.

You stand up and head toward another part of the deck. Just then, another explosion shakes the deck and throws you forward. You feel a blast of hot wind and see a huge firestorm coming at you. You cover your head as the flames reach you. But there is no escape. You are one of the 1,177 men from *Arizona* to die during the attack.

THE END

To follow another path, turn to page 11.
To read the conclusion, turn to page 103.

You rush toward your battle station. As you run, you see your friend Bob and grab his arm.

"Where are you going?" you yell over the roar of explosions, flames, and shouts.

"I heard an officer give the order to abandon ship!" he yells back. "I'm getting off this ship!"

A column of flames and smoke rises above the deck. You can feel the heat from the flames.

"Come with me!" Bob yells. "It's your only chance."

You hesitate. You have time to escape. But you don't feel right abandoning the ship without trying to fight back.

To continue to your battle station, turn to page **69**.

To try to escape, turn to page **71**.

You can't leave the man here, so you grab him by the feet and try to drag him. Officers and other sailors run past you, leaping over the man as more bombs explode above you.

You hear a loud blast, and *Arizona* shakes violently. Flames roar through the ship. You have to get away from them, and you can't drag the injured man with you. You take a deep breath and jump overboard.

Black smoke poured from burning battleships during the attack.

Turn the page.

A shout rings out from a small rescue boat nearby. A man reaches down and grabs your badly burned arm. "We'll get you fixed up, sailor," he says as he gently hauls you into the boat.

Eventually, the rescue boat lands on shore. You're taken to the hospital on Ford Island. Stretchers fill the parking lot, holding hundreds of wounded. There are only a few doctors and nurses examining the injured.

Hours later, you're put into a hospital bed, where you stay for several weeks. Your burns are bad, and you lost three fingers. When you are released, you are discharged from the military. You go back to your hometown to wait out the rest of the war.

THE END

To follow another path, turn to page 11.
To read the conclusion, turn to page 103.

No, you have to stay with the ship. "Go on, and good luck!" you say to Bob. He gives you a surprised look and then disappears into the smoke. You hope he makes it.

You turn and run. Soon you reach the storage area. Officers scream orders as you try to get the ammunition out and up to the deck. People run and shout, and it's hard to know exactly what to do. But you're strangely calm. You signed up to fight for America, and this is your chance.

Turn the page.

Suddenly, a bomb lands on the front of the ship, rocking it so hard that everyone falls to the deck. Then, a deafening blast fills the air. The fire instantly roars through the area.

You see everything around you burst into flames. You don't realize at first that you're on fire too. The pain lasts only a few seconds. Then it's all over. You've given your life to defend the United States.

To follow another path, turn to page 11.
To read the conclusion, turn to page 103.

Oklahoma sank next to *Maryland*.

You and Bob race to the deck. Bombs rip through the ship as you run. When you get there, you can't believe what you see. Flames and smoke are everywhere. People are running, planes are screaming overhead, and blasts fill the air.

Turn the page.

A huge explosion throws you high into the air. When you hit the deck, your leg crumples beneath you. You scream in pain and sink onto the deck. It is warm from the heat of the fires around you. You're covered in sweat, ashes, and blood. You don't see Bob anywhere.

You don't think you should stay here. But you're not sure you can make it off the boat. You try to stand, but the pain is too bad. You could crawl to the edge of the deck. Or you can stay here and hope someone rescues you.

To wait to be rescued, go to page 73.

To abandon ship, turn to page 74.

You think it's safer to stay here. You call out to several sailors running across the deck. Then your friend Tom appears out of the smoke. "I thought I heard your voice!" he yells. He picks you up and throws you over his shoulder. You almost faint from the pain. Tom carries you as fast as he can toward the railing. "There's a rescue boat out there," he shouts.

A huge explosion erupts around you, then another. The ship shakes violently, and Tom loses his balance. You both fall to the deck as a wall of fire roars toward you. There is no time to move. Even though the war has barely begun, for you, it's all over.

To follow another path, turn to page 11.
To read the conclusion, turn to page 103.

If you stay here, you'll die. You inch across the deck, groaning with pain as you drag your injured leg behind you. With a huge effort, you lift yourself over the railing and plunge into the water below.

The water is sticky with gasoline, oil, and blood, and soon you are too. Men are floating in the water all around you. Some of them are dead, burned so badly that you don't recognize them. A few, like you, are still alive. And still the bombs keep coming.

You feel yourself falling unconscious. "No!" you think, shaking yourself awake. If you pass out, you'll die.

Somewhere through the smoke, you think you hear voices calling. You could try to swim toward the voices. Or you can grab some debris and stay here, hoping someone will find you.

To try to swim, turn to page 76.

To grab something and hang on, turn to page 77.

You're pretty sure you can make it to the voices, so you start to swim. Pain instantly shoots up your leg. You struggle forward, trying not to faint. You can't see through the smoke.

The voices seem to be moving around, so you try to follow the sound. Just a little farther, and you'll be there. But you don't find anyone. You're very tired and in terrible pain. "I'll rest a few minutes, and then I'll try again," you think. With a sigh, you lie back in the water. Slowly, the pain goes away as you slip into unconsciousness and drown.

THE END

To follow another path, turn to page 11.
To read the conclusion, turn to page 103.

You grab a life preserver floating by and hang on tight. A few minutes later, rough hands grab you and pull you into a rescue boat.

"Am I going to make it?" you moan.

"Of course, sailor!" the man says. "You're going to be fine."

"Where are you taking me?" you ask. "Is anything left in the harbor?"

Rescuers in small boats were able to pull survivors from the water during the attack.

Turn the page.

The man frowns as he tucks a blanket around you. "Not much, from the looks of it," he says. "But you're alive, and that's what counts. We're taking you to *Solace*."

USS *Solace* is a hospital ship. It was not damaged in the attack. You'll be safe there.

You fall into unconsciousness. When you wake up, it's dark. You're in a soft, clean bed, and your wounds have been bandaged. You try to move, but your leg is in a heavy cast.

"Ah, you're awake," a nurse says, giving you a sip of water.

"*Arizona*?" you ask. "What happened to my ship?"

The nurse's eyes fill with tears. "Destroyed," she says. "The bombs hit the ammunition stores, which exploded. It tore the ship in two. You're very lucky to be alive." You lie back, stunned. The United States has no choice but to join in the war now.

After a few weeks in the hospital, you recover from your injuries. It's a good thing, because you've been itching to get to war since the attack.

The day you are released, you get orders to report to another ship, USS *Maryland*. This ship was only lightly damaged during the attack. Soon you'll be out to sea, a part of the U.S. forces in the South Pacific.

THE END

To follow another path, turn to page 11.
To read the conclusion, turn to page 103.

Beaches and warm weather attract many people to Hawaii.

CHAPTER 4

On the Shore

After finishing nursing school, you joined the military. You like the idea of being able to travel and see the world. You couldn't believe your luck when your first assignment was at a base in Hawaii.

Hawaii turns out to be as beautiful and interesting as you thought it would be. The only thing that spoils your enjoyment of your new home is talk of war. Today, though, war is far from your mind. It's a gorgeous Sunday morning, December 7. You have a rare day off.

Turn the page.

You're making coffee when you hear a strange noise. You look out your window and see a large fleet of planes flying fast and low over your house. "Someone should report those guys," you think. Pilots shouldn't disturb people on a Sunday. Then you notice the red sun symbol on the planes. "Those aren't our boys," you say out loud.

Before you have time to think, you hear the sound of bombs exploding in the distance. You run outside. The first columns of black smoke rise from the harbor.

Suddenly, people fill the streets. Shouts of "Attack!" echo through your neighborhood. You've got to get to the hospital. There will be wounded people, and every nurse will be needed.

You rush into your house and quickly change into your white nurse's uniform. Then you run back into the street, hoping you can find a ride to the hospital. A car screeches to a stop in front of you. It's one of your neighbors. He's a medic at one of the field hospitals.

"Please take me to the hospital!" you cry.

"Okay," the man replies. "But they also need help on the docks with the wounded men coming off the boats. I'm headed to the harbor."

You hesitate. You know they'll need you at the hospital. But you might be of help at the harbor too.

To go to the hospital, turn to page **84**.

To go with the medic to the harbor, turn to page **86**.

"I need to get to the hospital," you shout as you jump in the car. Your neighbor nods. It's not far to the hospital, but the drive seems to take forever. Smoke and the smell of burning debris fill the air.

At the hospital, you jump out of the car. "Good luck," you call to your neighbor as he speeds away toward the harbor. You can hear the loud rumble of planes overhead and the crash of bombs as they hit their targets. You run into the hospital.

"Thank goodness you're here!" says a doctor you've never met. "Many doctors and nurses are away at a meeting. We're short-staffed."

"What can I do?" you ask, looking around.

"Several first aid stations are being set up near the ships," he says, looking worried. "They're going to fix up the less serious injuries. But the badly injured patients will need to come here. We need people to drive them."

It seems that you're needed everywhere. You can be useful either at the shore or in the hospital. Which do you decide to do?

To volunteer to drive the injured, turn to page **88**.

To stay at the hospital, turn to page **96**.

It only takes you a few minutes to get to the shore. The medic gives you some first aid supplies and then disappears into the smoke.

You look around, unsure of where to go. The noise is deafening. Shouts, screams, and explosions fill the air. The sky is black with smoke. You duck as debris and bits of flaming metal fly through the air.

Crews attempted to put out the fires on *West Virginia* and other ships in the harbor.

A giant explosion suddenly rips through the harbor, violently shaking the ground. You fall to the ground just as an enormous ball of fire shoots from *Arizona*. Smoke and fire consume the battleship. Several other ships have caught fire and are burning.

You finally tear yourself away from the horrible sight of the destroyed ship and run to the water. Hundreds of men are floating in the water. On shore, several people are trying to get the injured to safety. You quickly begin helping the injured out of the filthy water. Many of them are badly burned. Breaking open your first aid supplies, you try to do what you can. Soon, you see a ship on the water. It's *Solace*, a hospital ship.

To help the doctors aboard Solace, *turn to page* **92**.

To stay on the shore, turn to page **94**.

"I can drive the injured," you offer. "We can't help anyone if they can't get to the hospital."

The doctor nods and hands you the keys to a maintenance truck. You jump in and race toward the harbor. Japanese planes fill the sky above the battleships. Bombs come down like hail. People are running everywhere. The smoke makes the sky as dark as night.

USS *California* was badly damaged in the attack.

You arrive at the water's edge just as rescue workers are pulling victims from the harbor. You and two medics carefully lay several injured men in the back of the truck. Without a word, you speed to the hospital. There you help carry the injured to the emergency room. Then you quickly drive back to the harbor.

You make several runs to and from the hospital. The back of the truck is filled with injured men. As you load one badly burned man into the truck, he weakly grabs your hand.

"What . . . where . . ." he whispers.

"You're being taken to the hospital, sailor," you say. "The Japanese have attacked Pearl Harbor."

Turn the page.

The man groans. "I was in the gun turrets when the bombs hit," he says. "Next thing I knew, I was in the water. Fire everywhere. Don't know how I got there."

"Try to relax," you say. You try not to look at his severely burned hands and face. Instead, you smile reassuringly. "We're going to get you fixed right up."

As you leave for the hospital, you notice a Japanese plane flying very low overhead. You quickly swerve down a side street. A few seconds later, you hear a huge explosion. There's a plume of fire and smoke near the hospital.

When you get to the hospital, you're relieved to see that the bomb didn't hit the building. But a nearby building was destroyed. The wreckage of a Japanese plane burns in front of the building.

This Japanese plane crashed near Pearl Harbor during the attack.

"What happened?" you call to a soldier running across the parking lot.

"He crashed!" he answers. "We're lucky he didn't hit the hospital!"

You agree. If he'd hit the hospital . . . you don't want to think about it. Right now, you've got a job to do. The hospital is going to need every pair of hands available.

Turn to page **96**.

Quickly, you board a small rescue boat from *Solace*. It's heading toward *Arizona* to rescue the injured there. When you arrive, you and the other rescuers climb aboard. You don't have a lot of time. The ship is on fire, and the smoke is so thick that you can't breathe. You can feel the heat of the metal deck through your shoes.

"Come with me," one of the rescuers calls to you. You run toward two sailors who are lying facedown on the deck. All around you, sailors are abandoning ship, but you're not going anywhere. You and the other rescuers find several injured men and carry them to the rescue boat.

Back at *Solace,* you help unload the injured. Before you're finished, a doctor comes up to you.

"Nurses are needed at the hospital," he says. "They're shorthanded."

"But we're shorthanded here too," you reply. Now you're not sure what to do.

To go back to the hospital, turn to page **96**.

To stay on Solace, *turn to page* **100**.

You can be of more use here on shore. There is blood, oil, and gasoline everywhere. The attack finally ends. But your work is just starting.

As the men are rescued from the filthy, oily water, you bandage their wounds and try to make them comfortable. Trucks, jeeps, and ambulances come and go. You help load the injured men for their trip to the hospital.

Ambulances like this one carried victims to hospitals on Pearl Harbor.

Men have been hit by bits of metal and other debris. Some are horribly burned and injured. But sailors who were wearing long pants and shirts have only minor burns. Those wearing shorts and T-shirts have worse injuries.

Over the next few days, you help care for hundreds of people injured in the attack. You're too busy working to pay much attention when Congress declares war on December 8.

About a week after the attack, you get new orders for duty on USS *President Coolidge*. You will care for patients who are being transported from other places. You wonder what will happen next. No one knows how the war will turn out, but you are determined to do whatever you can to help.

To follow another path, turn to page 11.
To read the conclusion, turn to page 103.

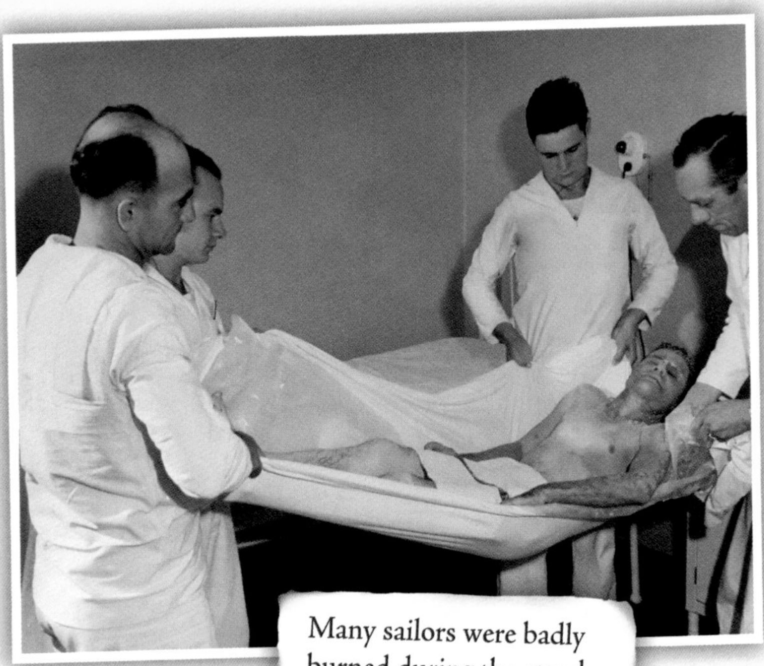

Many sailors were badly burned during the attack.

The hospital overflows with injured men. You barely have time to wash your hands before you're called to help. Most of the men have been terribly burned by the fires on the ships. You and the other nurses bandage their wounds and give them medicine to ease the pain. Cots are quickly set up in the hallways, and soon they are filled too.

Some time later, you notice that the number of injured coming in is slowing down. "What's going on?" you ask a passing soldier.

"Attack is long over," he replies tiredly. "They came in two waves. The first one pretty much destroyed our battleships and planes. We managed to get a few shots in when they came back an hour later."

You spend the rest of the day caring for the injured and the dying. As you wash the face of one young sailor, he wakes up and looks at you. "Where are Jim and Billy?" he asks.

"I don't know," you're forced to say. "What happened to you?"

Turn the page.

The sailor looks away. "We were on *Oklahoma*," he says. "Never saw so much smoke and fire in my life. Jim and Billy were trapped below deck. Some other guys and I tried to open the hatch, but it wouldn't budge. Then everything went dark."

"Both your legs are broken, but you'll be fine," you tell him.

Many of the sailors at Pearl Harbor were young men.

The man's eyes fill with tears. As you leave him, you hope that he'll find his friends someday. But you know he probably won't.

By nightfall, you're exhausted. After a few hours of rest, you're back at work. Someone turns on a radio. You hear President Roosevelt's declaration of war. The news is terrifying, but you're glad that the United States is going to defend itself against this terrible attack.

You receive orders to remain at Pearl Harbor for now. There is talk that the Japanese might try to invade, so you will be needed here. The world has changed, and you don't know what will happen next. Nobody does.

To follow another path, turn to page 11.
To read the conclusion, turn to page 103.

"I'll stay," you say. "I can do just as much good here as I can at the hospital."

The doctor smiles. "Thank you," he says.

You work for hours. When you finally stop for a minute, something seems very odd. Then it hits you. It's quiet. There are no more bombs or explosions. You didn't even notice when the attack ended. You sink onto a chair, exhausted from the day. It's dusk. A weary nurse notices you and walks over.

"You've been such a great help," she says. "Why don't you go home and get some rest? There's still a lot of work to be done, and we'll need fresh nurses tomorrow."

You nod. A small boat is leaving for the shore, and you climb aboard. Soon, you're making your way toward home.

The battleships *Cassin* and *Downes* were destroyed.

In the fading light, you see the destruction all around you. Several battleships are still burning. Piles of twisted metal lie everywhere. It's hard to believe that anyone survived this attack. You realize that the United States can no longer stay out of this war. You're afraid, but you're determined to do your part for your country.

THE END

To follow another path, turn to page 11.
To read the conclusion, turn to page 103.

On December 8, 1941, President Franklin D. Roosevelt asked Congress to declare war on Japan.

CHAPTER 5

Remember Pearl Harbor

The attack on December 7, 1941, took the world by surprise. The attack began just before 8:00 in the morning. By 10:00, it was over. Before the attack, the United States was at peace, determined not to join the war in Europe. By the time the last Japanese bomber pilot flew away, everything had changed.

The next day, December 8, President Roosevelt delivered one of his most famous speeches. He called December 7, 1941, "a date which will live in infamy." He asked Congress to declare war on Japan. His request was granted.

By all accounts, the attack was a success for the Japanese. They crippled the U.S. Navy. In all, the Japanese sank or severely damaged 18 American ships. The Japanese destroyed 188 American aircraft and damaged 159 others. At least 2,400 Americans died.

On the other hand, the Japanese lost only 29 airplanes. Only 55 Japanese airmen were killed. They also lost five midget submarines. Of the 10 crewmen on the midget submarines, nine died. One was captured and held as a prisoner of war.

But the Japanese failed to destroy the three American aircraft carriers normally stationed at Pearl Harbor. USS *Enterprise* and USS *Lexington* were delivering planes to nearby islands. The third, USS *Saratoga,* had gone to San Diego for repairs.

In the coming months, all but three of the American ships damaged in the attack were repaired. Only *Arizona, Oklahoma,* and *Utah* were completely lost. In just a year, the U.S. fleet was back to its full strength.

The Pearl Harbor attack united the American people against Japan and the Axis powers. The United States joined with the Soviet Union, Great Britain, and other European countries to form the Allied forces. Together, they faced the huge Axis armies in both Europe and the South Pacific.

At home, Americans were afraid. Many cities enforced blackouts at night to avoid enemy bombing. Thousands of Japanese Americans on the West Coast were removed from their homes. They were forced to live in internment camps under the watchful eye of the government.

The sunken *Arizona* remains at the bottom of Pearl Harbor below the memorial.

In June 1942, the Battle of Midway in the Pacific Ocean was a turning point in the war. At that battle, U.S. forces defeated the Japanese Navy. From then on, the United States had the advantage. Japan never completely recovered its sea forces.

In August 1945, the United States dropped two atomic bombs on Japan. The first destroyed the city of Hiroshima. The second fell on the city of Nagasaki. Within weeks, the Japanese stopped fighting. The war was over.

Pearl Harbor is still an important military base due to its location in the Pacific Ocean. Almost from the day of the attack, people wanted to create a memorial to the people who died at Pearl Harbor. In 1962, former President Dwight Eisenhower dedicated the *Arizona* Memorial. It was built on the water above the wreckage of *Arizona*, which can still be seen today.

TIME LINE

September 1, 1939 — World War II begins.

September 27, 1940 — Germany, Italy, and Japan agree to form the Axis powers.

December 7, 1941

3:42 a.m. — A Japanese submarine is spotted near Pearl Harbor.

6:15 a.m. — The first wave of Japanese attackers heads to Oahu.

6:45 a.m. — A Japanese submarine is sunk outside the entrance to Pearl Harbor.

7:15 a.m. — The second attack wave takes off from Japanese aircraft carriers.

7:49 a.m. — Commander Mitsuo Fuchida gives the signal to attack.

7:55 a.m. — Telegraph operators on Ford Island send out the first reports of the attack.

8:01 a.m. — *Oklahoma* and *West Virginia* are hit.

8:06 a.m. — The first bomb hits *Arizona*.

8:10 a.m. — *Arizona* is destroyed.

9:02 a.m. — The second wave of Japanese bombers attack Pearl Harbor.

9:27 a.m. — *Cassin* overturns onto *Downes*.

9:30 a.m. — *Shaw* explodes.

9:45 a.m. — Japanese planes begin returning to their aircraft carriers. The attack is over.

December 8, 1941 — The United States, Great Britain, and Canada declare war on Japan.

June 4–7, 1942 — American naval forces defeat Japan's fleet at the Battle of Midway.

February–March 1945 — The United States defeats Japanese forces at the Battle of Iwo Jima.

May 7, 1945 — Germany surrenders, ending World War II in Europe.

August 6, 1945 — The United States drops the first atomic bomb on the Japanese city of Hiroshima.

August 9, 1945 — The world's second atomic bomb destroys the Japanese city of Nagasaki.

August 14, 1945 — Japan agrees to surrender.

September 2, 1945 — Japanese officials sign the surrender document, officially ending World War II in the Pacific.

Other Paths to Explore

In this book, you've seen how the events experienced at Pearl Harbor on December 7, 1941, look different from three points of view.

Perspectives on history are as varied as the people who lived it. You can explore other paths on your own to learn more about what happened. Seeing history from many points of view is an important part of understanding it.

Here are some ideas for other Pearl Harbor attack points of view to explore:

- A few American fighter pilots were able to take off during the attack. What was it like to take on the Japanese fighter planes in the sky?
- More than 80 civilians were killed or injured during the attack. What would it have been like to live in Honolulu or nearby cities during the attack?
- Before the attack, Japan launched five midget submarines toward Pearl Harbor. Each vessel carried two men each. Only one of the men survived. What would it have been like to try to sneak into Pearl Harbor aboard a small submarine?

WORLD WAR II:

AN INTERACTIVE HISTORY ADVENTURE

BY ELIZABETH RAUM

CONSULTANT:
WILLIAM O. OLDSON, FOUNDER AND DIRECTOR
INSTITUTE ON WORLD WAR II AND THE HUMAN EXPERIENCE
FLORIDA STATE UNIVERSITY

Table of Contents

About Your Adventure

YOU are living in the late 1930s. More than 20 years have passed since World War I. Now conflicts in Europe and Japan are building up again. Will there be another world war?

In this book, you'll explore how the choices people made meant the difference between life and death. The events you'll experience happened to real people.

Chapter One sets the scene. Then you choose which path to read. Follow the directions at the bottom of each page. The choices you make will change your outcome. After you finish one path, go back and read the others for new perspectives and more adventures.

YOU CHOOSE the path you take through history.

Many Germans saluted Adolf Hitler as the leader of their country.

War!

"Look!" your brother says, holding up the newspaper on September 1, 1939. In black letters are the words "German Army Invades Poland."

Germany was not pleased with the peace that followed World War I (1914–1918). The country lost the war, and many Germans believed they were treated unfairly.

Adolf Hitler became the leader of Germany in 1933. He and his political party, the Nazis, blame Germany's problems on the last war. They also blame the Jews, a group of people descended from ancient Hebrews. Hitler believes the Jews are a weaker race than the white German race. "A stronger race will drive out the weak," he writes.

Turn the page.

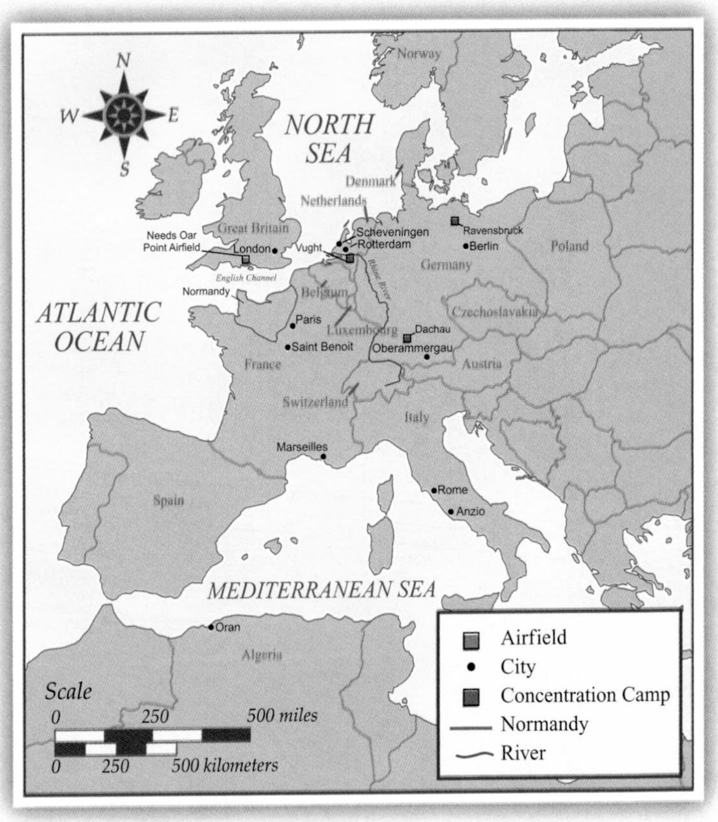

Hitler promises to make Germany powerful again. He began in 1938 by taking over Austria. In March 1939, Hitler seized Czechoslovakia. And now his army has invaded Poland.

"There's fighting in Asia too," your brother says. "The Japanese are attacking China."

The leader of Italy, Benito Mussolini, vows to help Germany gain power in Europe. In 1940, Japan joins Germany and Italy to form the Axis powers.

Poland, Great Britain, France, India, Australia, and New Zealand hope to stop the Axis. Together they are known as the Allied forces, or Allies.

"Will there be another world war?" you ask.

"I'm afraid so," your father says. Sooner or later, you'll have to decide what role to play.

To join the forces fighting the Germans in the Netherlands, turn to page **121.**

To sign up for the Canadian military, turn to page **151.**

To serve with the American armed forces, turn to page **177.**

German bombs destroyed the city of Rotterdam, the Netherlands, in May 1940.

War in the Netherlands

Early Friday morning, May 10, 1940, you awake to the sound of popping noises filling the air. "What's going on?" you ask.

"Those are German planes!" your brother shouts, pointing to the sky. "They're shooting at our planes."

"But the Netherlands is neutral. We aren't part of the war."

"That doesn't matter to Hitler," your brother says. "First he attacked Poland, then Norway and Denmark. Now he's coming after us."

Turn the page.

The Germans are heavily armed with tanks and bombers. The small Dutch Army has no tanks. Their planes are old. They ride bicycles and carry outdated guns. Outnumbered and outmatched, the Dutch Army does its best to hold off the Germans. After three days, the Germans control most of the country. But the major cities are still under Dutch control.

On May 14, Germans drop bomb after bomb on the city of Rotterdam. The city is destroyed. More than 900 people, including your cousin, are killed in the attack. The next day, the Dutch government surrenders to the Germans.

That night, your family gathers around the radio. London's radio station, the BBC, reports that Queen Wilhelmina and the Dutch government have left the Netherlands for England. "Why has she left us in our time of need?" you ask.

"She must have good reasons, my daughter. Someday we'll understand," Father says.

When German soldiers march through the streets, you stand on the sidewalk and sob. Your cousin is dead, and your country is no longer free.

Some of your neighbors support the Germans by joining the Dutch Nazi Party. Others welcome German soldiers into their homes. Not you and your family. You want nothing to do with the Nazis.

Soon the Nazis' secret police, the Gestapo, begin making rules. First they make it illegal to listen to the BBC. Then they order citizens to turn in their radios.

"We'll keep our radio," your father says.

Turn the page.

It's dangerous. If the Germans find the radio, your father could be arrested.

"They won't find it," he says. He cuts a hole in the wall. Then he moves the radio, which is the size of a small dresser, into that space. A bookshelf hides the lower half. He hangs a mirror over the top part.

Every night, you listen to broadcasts from the Dutch government in England. It is the only news you trust.

Your brother begins a secret newspaper to report what you hear on the radio. "Will you help me deliver copies to the neighbors?" he asks.

It is dangerous work. If you are caught, you will be arrested. And the Nazis kill traitors.

To help deliver the newspapers, go to page **125**.

To refuse to help, turn to page **127**.

Queen Wilhelmina of the Netherlands was forced to flee to London at the beginning of World War II.

"Of course, I'll help," you say.

"Be careful to avoid the homes of Nazi supporters," he reminds you.

You and your brother join a group of young people who resist the Nazis. You go out after dark and write OZO, the Dutch abbreviation for "Orange will conquer," on nearby walls. The Germans have forbidden any mention of the royal family or their royal color, orange.

Turn the page.

One day, a German soldier stops you as you are walking home. "What is this jewelry you are wearing?" he says. He points to a 10-cent silver coin pinned to your shirt. The coin has a picture of Queen Wilhelmina on the front. "It is against the law to display the queen's picture," he says. He tears the coin away. "Go quickly before I arrest you. I'll be watching you."

You tell your brother what happened. "That's enough," he says. "I'm going to England. I'll help the queen and the Dutch government take the Netherlands back from the Germans. Come with me."

You've heard others talk of going to England. You're tempted to go, but your parents are getting old. If you leave, they'll be alone.

To go to England, turn to page **128**.

To stay with your parents, turn to page **130**.

"It's too dangerous," you say.

"If you feel that way, it's better you don't help," your brother answers. "Fear won't help the resistance."

You take classes at the university. You try to ignore German soldiers in the streets. If you just mind your own business, everything will be all right. Whenever you hear planes overhead, you pray that it is Allied soldiers coming to save the Netherlands.

In April 1943, the Germans force all university students to sign a loyalty oath. Those who don't sign must leave school.

To refuse to sign, turn to page **129**.

To sign, turn to page **149**.

"Go to England," your father says. "We are old. We'll be fine here, but you young people will be safer in England."

You go with your brother to a farming area near the coast. On a moonless night, a man you trust guides you to a rickety old boat. Seven of you will use it to cross the English Channel.

"There are German lookout posts along the entire Dutch coast. Go directly out to sea. And be careful," your guide says.

"I'm worried," you say. "I'm not a good swimmer. If the boat sinks, I'll drown."

The guide invites you to stay on the coast. "We do what we can to help from here."

"It's up to you," your brother says. "I'm going."

To stay in the Netherlands, turn to page **133**.

To go to England, turn to page **146**.

One of your professors declares, "We must resist this demand to sign an oath." He's your favorite professor and a man of courage. You refuse to sign.

A classmate takes you aside. "I feel I can trust you," she says. "We need young women to help in the resistance. Most of our young men have been shipped to work camps in the Soviet Union. It's dangerous work, but we try to get information to England. We also rescue Allied pilots. Come to the coast with me."

To help in the resistance, turn to page **133**.

To stay in the city with your parents, turn to **148**.

"I'll stay. I won't leave my homeland," you say.

Soon the Germans make laws that discriminate against Jewish people. Jews cannot go to the park. They cannot play sports. They can't even walk on the sunny side of the street. Jews are beaten, and their property is destroyed.

By late 1941, many Jews know that they must leave the country or go into hiding. If they don't, they risk being killed by the Nazis. Leaving the Netherlands is impossible. Germany controls all of the surrounding land.

Some Jews hide in apartments or homes in the cities. Farms make even better hiding places. Many Dutch farmers are willing to place their own families in danger to hide Jews.

You join Group HEIN, named after the Dutch initials for the phrase, "helping others in need." The group helps Jews hide from the Nazis.

More than 20 Jews crowded into this tiny bunker to hide from the Germans.

Your job is to bike from farm to farm. You pick up letters at one farm and deliver them to the next. The Germans have taken most bikes. They use the parts for weapons, especially the rubber tires. You ride an ancient bike with rolled garden hoses for tires.

Like others in the group, you use a false name and a fake ID. That way, if you are found, the Nazis will not hurt your family.

Turn the page.

One day, as you bike from one farm to another, you spot a German checkpoint ahead. You think about turning back. But your fake ID is new. The Jewish printer who made it does good work. Do you dare go through the roadblock? If you turn back, you'll have to go miles out of your way.

To go through the checkpoint, turn to page **141**.

To turn back, turn to page **144**.

Your country needs your help in the resistance. The group's headquarters are at a farm near the North Sea. A powerful radio sends messages back and forth from England. One night, the group gathers around the radio operator. He receives a secret message.

"Allied planes will fly over tomorrow night," he says. "They'll drop weapons and bundles of an illegal newspaper called *The Flying Dutchman*."

You go with the group to a nearby field. Two men signal the planes with flashlights.

Something lands by your feet. You grab the bundle of newspapers. Four strong men carry a trunk filled with guns. "Come quickly!" one of them says. "We'll go to a safe house in town."

Turn the page.

But a German soldier stands guard on the bridge into town. One of the men tells you to go talk to the soldier. "While he's busy trying to impress you, we'll sneak past him."

"No," another says. "That's too dangerous. We'll hide in the shed back in the field and try again another night."

To return to the field to hide, go to page **135**.

To volunteer to distract the guard, turn to page **137**.

It's safer to hide. German soldiers must have seen the Allied planes. They are searching for you. It is a miracle they don't find you. By 4:00 in the morning, the German patrols are gone. You haul the guns and newspapers back to the farm.

You hide everything in a farm wagon beneath a load of stinky cow manure. German soldiers won't bother to dig through the manure looking for hidden weapons. The farmer delivers the papers to a safe house in town.

By 1943, food is scarce in the Netherlands. Everyone uses ration cards to buy groceries. It's a fair way to distribute food. But people who are hiding cannot get ration cards. They depend on fake ration cards and false ID cards. As a Dutch girl, you have freedom to travel. Your job is to carry fake papers to people in hiding.

Turn the page.

Today you must take forged papers to a farm where 20 people are hiding. Some are Jewish. Some are Dutch men who have refused to join the German Army or work in German factories. Without ration cards, these people will starve.

As you bike along, you see a German roadblock up ahead. Since the Germans arrived, everyone must carry official identification papers. Your papers are fake. You use a false name. If you are arrested using your real name, your parents might be put in jail too.

You've never used your fake papers before. If there is an error, you could be arrested. Do you trust your papers enough to go through the roadblock, or should you turn back?

To go through the checkpoint, turn to page **141**.

To turn back, turn to page **144**.

German troops guarded streets during the German occupation of the Netherlands.

"I'll distract the guard," you whisper. One of the men takes your newspapers. You walk along the bridge. "Halt!" the guard says in German. He asks for your identification.

Slowly, you reach into your pocket. The first pocket is empty.

Turn the page.

"Now!" the soldier roars. You smile sweetly at him and shrug as if you don't mean to cause harm. Finally you hand over your papers. You have managed to turn the guard so that his back is to the bridge. You see your friends sneak safely past. He hands you back your papers. "Where are you going?" he asks.

"To my aunt's house. Soldiers took my bicycle, so I had to walk. It took me longer than I expected."

"I will walk you to your aunt's house," the soldier says. But you have no aunt in this town.

To let the soldier walk you to town, go to page **139**.

To run away, turn to page **143**.

You wait for the soldier to walk with you. What can you do?

"Which house?" the German asks. You point to a narrow house nestled between two bigger, taller houses. "There," you say, praying that whoever is there will take you in.

The German marches to the door and knocks. An elderly woman answers. She looks from you to the soldier.

"Auntie!" you say, trying to keep your voice from shaking. Can she understand that you need her protection?

She does! She reaches out and hugs you. The soldier turns to leave. Once he is gone, your "aunt" shuts the door. You thank her for her kindness.

"It's nothing," she says. "Go in peace." You slip out a back door and join the others at a safe house.

Turn the page.

It becomes more and more difficult to get food. Everyone must use ration cards at stores to purchase food. But people who are hiding, whether they are Jewish or Dutch, do not have cards. Luckily, a Jewish man who is hiding at a nearby farm makes cards that look real. Your job is to pick up the ration cards from him.

One day, you are biking back to the secret headquarters. You have an envelope full of false ration cards. But up ahead, you spot a German checkpoint. If they catch you with the cards, they'll put you in prison. You could toss the cards in a nearby ditch and go through the checkpoint. Or you could turn around. Then you would be able to deliver the ration cards. But you'd have to bike miles out of the way.

To go through the checkpoint, go to page **141**.

To turn around, turn to page **144**.

Your ID card is new, and the forger does good work, so you go ahead toward the checkpoint. But when the Gestapo officer checks your ID, he laughs and calls another officer over.

"Come with me," he says. He can tell your ID is fake. "You are under arrest."

You are sent by train to a prison in Scheveningen. This city is on the coast of the North Sea. There are two sections of the camp. One is for Jews, and one is for political prisoners like you.

Every Tuesday and Thursday, more Jews arrive. The Germans are rounding them up from all over the Netherlands. From here, the Germans send them to Poland. You hear the Jewish children crying. How terrible it must be for entire families to be jailed just because they are Jewish.

Turn the page.

Female prisoners were forced to work at Ravensbruck concentration camp.

In June 1944, you are moved to the Vught concentration camp. In Vught, you make rope for the German Army. Without enough food, many women become sick. On September 6, 1944, you are sent to the Ravensbruck concentration camp in Germany. This camp is even worse than Vught. You die there of starvation on May 4, 1945. It is only four days before the war in Europe ends.

To follow another path, turn to page 119.
To read the conclusion, turn to page 211.

The second the soldier looks away, you run. You hear a bullet whiz by your ear. It will be better if the soldier shoots you than takes you alive. If you are dead, you cannot tell secrets that will lead the Germans to find others in the resistance. You keep running. Another bullet whizzes past. Then another. The fourth hits its mark. You fall to the ground and bleed to death in the street. Your only comfort is that no one will discover your secrets.

To follow another path, turn to page 119.
To read the conclusion, turn to page 211.

It's safer to bike back the way you came. You are tired by the time you reach the farm where you live.

The next day, gunfire and bombing wake you up. You join others who are hiding in the basement. "We don't know what's happening," a young mother says, clutching her baby in her arms.

"All we can do is wait," you tell her. "And pray."

After three days of constant noise, there is silence. What is happening? Someone has to go see.

To remain inside, go to page **145**.

To volunteer to go outside, turn to page **147**.

The farmer says he will go. His wife begs him to wait. They have four young children. He brushes aside her concern and leaves. Then you hear gunshots.

You rush to the door. The farmer stands next to the house, safe. A German soldier lies dead in the yard. An Allied soldier stands over him, holding a rifle. You rush forward and hug the soldier. "Thank you. Thank you. You have come at last!" you say.

Other soldiers march past the farm. At long last, the Netherlands is free. The soldiers have more fighting ahead of them, but for you, the war is finally over.

THE END

To follow another path, turn to page 119.
To read the conclusion, turn to page 211.

"We'll be fine," your brother says. "It's what Father wants."

You climb into the crowded little boat. Then a German submarine, called a U-boat, appears in the distance. What if they see you? But the U-boat disappears beneath the surface.

Just when you feel safe, you notice that your feet are wet. The boat is leaking. You try to bail out water with a small tin cup. But the water keeps pouring into the boat. Some of the others dive into the sea to try to swim home. But it's too far for you. "You go," you say to your brother, but he refuses. You die together in the cold water off the coast of your beloved Netherlands.

THE END

To follow another path, turn to page 119.
To read the conclusion, turn to page 211.

Citizens in Utrecht, the Netherlands, welcomed Allied troops to their city in May 1945.

You rush outside. Tanks roll by. Canadian soldiers march behind them. They are searching for any remaining German troops. "We'll clear them out," a soldier tells you. You run and tell the others. Everyone pours out of the house. It is the first time in months that they have been able to wander outside. They cry for joy. So do you!

THE END

To follow another path, turn to page 119.
To read the conclusion, turn to page 211.

You stay in the city to help your parents. Every day, you worry that the Gestapo will come after you and your parents. You've done nothing wrong. But your brother's actions with the resistance group have put you in danger.

By the winter of 1944, food is scarce. You, your mother, and your father have ration cards. But even with the cards, there's not enough food to go around. You even dig up Father's favorite tulip bulbs and cook them. They taste like potatoes.

Finally in April 1945, Allied troops march into your city. The Germans have lost. On New Year's Day, 1946, you get bad news. Your brother died in Germany's Dachau concentration camp in January 1945. You'll never forget him or his bravery.

THE END

To follow another path, turn to page 119.
To read the conclusion, turn to page 211.

Some people speak against signing the pledge. But your parents keep saying that the war will soon be over. "We've already lost your brother to the resistance," they say. "We need to know that one of our children is safe." You sign.

Food grows scarce at the end of the war. But thanks to your ration cards, you survive. At last, in April 1945, Allied tanks roll into town. The Germans surrender. You are free.

But your joy disappears when you learn that your brother was captured. He was tried as a traitor and shipped to a concentration camp in Germany. He died there. Everyone calls him a hero. You wish you could have been as brave as he was.

To follow another path, turn to page 119.
To read the conclusion, turn to page 211.

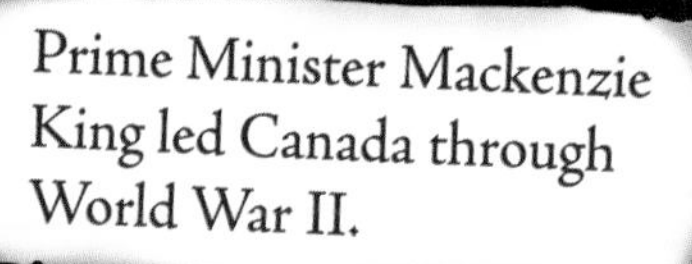

Prime Minister Mackenzie King led Canada through World War II.

CHAPTER 3

Canada Fights for Victory

On September 3, 1939, Great Britain, France, Australia, and New Zealand declare war on Germany. On September 10, the Canadian Parliament also declares war on Germany. You listen to Prime Minister Mackenzie King's speech on the radio. "I appeal to my fellow Canadians to unite in a national effort to save from destruction all that makes life itself worth living," he says.

King's speech inspires you. Canada needs volunteers to serve in the armed forces.

To join the Winnipeg Grenadiers, an army division, turn to page **152**.

To join the Royal Canadian Air Force, turn to page **155**.

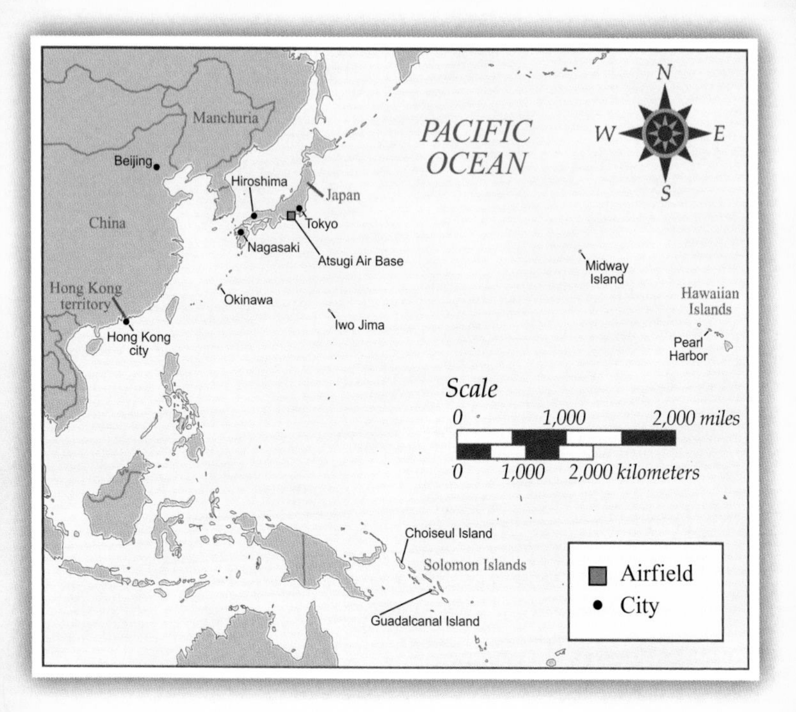

On September 30, 1939, you sign on with the Winnipeg Grenadiers. In May, you go to Jamaica to guard German prisoners of war (POWs) being held there.

In October 1941, your unit joins men from the Royal Rifles, a Signal Corps unit from Quebec. You are assigned to the cargo ship Awatea. There are 1,975 soldiers aboard from all over Canada.

"We're going to the British territory of Hong Kong," an officer announces. "Japanese forces are threatening to invade Hong Kong island."

On November 16, 1941, the ship docks in the city of Hong Kong. You begin training to learn how to survive on the mountainous island.

Early on December 8, sirens wail. Japanese planes bomb the harbor. You fire back. "Why are they bombing?" you ask.

"Yesterday the Japanese attacked Pearl Harbor in Hawaii. Canada, the United States, and Great Britain declared war on the Japanese," an officer says. "We're the first Canadians to join the fight."

The Japanese try to take over Mount Butler on Hong Kong Island. On December 19, Sergeant Major J. R. Osborn leads you into the dark fog to defend the island.

Turn the page.

For three hours, you fight the Japanese troops. But they outnumber you, and they have better weapons. You take cover in a ditch. "Stay down," an officer yells. "You'll be safe if you don't leave this trench. Help is on the way."

Japanese soldiers toss grenades at you. Sergeant Major Osborn catches several and throws them back, saving the lives of his men. Then a grenade falls where he can't get it.

"Grenade!" he shouts as he falls on top of it. The grenade explodes, killing Osborn. Just then, you hear a friend yell, "Help me! I've been shot."

To follow orders and stay in the trench, turn to page **156.**

To go to your friend's aid, turn to page **173.**

You decide to become a pilot and join the Royal Canadian Air Force (RCAF). You report to Elementary Flying Training School at Chatham, New Brunswick. The RCAF needs pilots as badly as it needs planes. You learn to fly whatever old planes are available. You earn your wings at the No. 9 Service Flying Training School at Summerside, Prince Edward Island. Then it's off to Scotland for more training.

British pilots introduce you to a new plane, the Hawker Typhoon. It's a low-wing, single-seater fighter plane with extra armor.

"We call them Tiffies," a British pilot tells you. "We're still testing them. Want to take a test flight?" You hesitate. There are rumors that the Tiffies have problems.

To take the test flight, turn to page **158**.

To refuse, turn to page **160**.

Allied soldiers surrendered to Japanese forces in the Pacific.

You follow orders and wait in the protected trench. An Australian soldier pulls your wounded friend to safety. The Japanese call for you to surrender. You have no choice. Before you surrender, you take apart your rifle and throw the parts into the jungle.

On December 25, after more than 17 days of fighting, all of Hong Kong falls to the Japanese. You are now a prisoner of war.

After several days, the Japanese move you to your abandoned barracks. The Japanese have taken over your camp and turned it into a prison. The buildings are a mess. Everything has been looted. The townspeople took everything they could use.

Food is scarce. Supper is just three very hard biscuits, called hardtack. You also have a few spoonfuls of canned beef called bully.

In basic training, you were told to escape if you were captured. One day, the Japanese commander brings you a paper. It says that you will promise not to try to escape. He wants you to sign it. Everyone seems to be signing. It's the smart thing to do. But isn't it your duty to escape?

To sign the promise, turn to page **174.**

To refuse to sign, turn to page **175.**

"I'll test the plane," you say. You soar over the countryside. Then you begin to yawn. Why are you feeling so sleepy? You struggle to stay awake, but you can't. Your body goes limp, and you lose control of the plane. The plane crashes into a farm field.

The farmer who finds you is amazed you're still alive. "What happened?" he asks. But you don't know.

It takes engineers several weeks to find out what happened. A gas called carbon monoxide leaked into the cockpit from the engine. The gas acted like a sleeping pill. That's not the only problem with the Tiffies. Several other pilots die when wings fall off and engines fail during flights. To your relief, engineers finally solve the problems.

You begin flying across the English Channel to patrol the coast of Europe. German beach patrols aim guns at the sky. Unless you stay high, you'll be hit. When you get the signal from your commander, you lower the plane to 4,000 feet. Then you drop two 1,000-pound bombs. You see them explode and hope they hit enemy targets.

As you head home, an enemy aircraft follows. You zigzag to avoid his firing guns. Then you hear the screech of metal tearing. Is it a wing? An engine? One of your buddies covers you from behind. "Got him!" he yells over the radio. Your plane shakes, but it's still flying. Maybe you can make it home. But what if you can't?

To parachute out, turn to page **163**.

To fly back to England, turn to page **172**.

You decide to let others test the planes, and you're glad you did. You hear of wings falling off and engines failing during test flights. Several pilots are killed.

In time, engineers work out the problems with the Hawker Typhoons. You begin flying over the English Channel, bombing German supply boats.

Bombing boats is not enough to win the war. Troops must land in France and attack the Germans on the ground. In April 1944, you go to an airfield at Needs Oar Point in England. From there, you join 11,000 planes flying to France.

You are clearing the way for thousands of soldiers to land on the beaches of Normandy. This region is in northern France. Countless bombs destroy radar and communication stations. The rat-tat-tat of antiaircraft guns fills the air.

Troops arrived on French beaches on June 6, 1944.

By 5:00 in the morning on June 6, 1944, 5,000 boats wait offshore. Troops storm the beach. The landing is called D-Day. By nightfall, 156,000 Allied troops have reached shore.

The Germans are surprised, but they fight back. German soldiers begin firing on the Allies from hills above the beach. Many British, Canadian, and American soldiers lose their lives on the beaches of Normandy.

Turn the page.

Allied forces flew Hawker Typhoons during battles over France.

On June 29, you are flying one of 10 Typhoons over France. At least 20 German Messerschmitt Bf 109s are chasing you. Rat-tat-tat! You fire back and climb higher. Enemy gunfire hits your plane. You go into a spin. You pull out of the spin and manage to keep the plane in the air. Then the engine begins to vibrate.

To parachute out, turn to page **166**.

To try to reach the airstrip at the beach, turn to page **167**.

You parachute out over enemy territory and land in a farm field. You check your escape kit. It contains a water bottle, chocolate, and pills to keep you awake. It also has a needle and thread, a fishhook, a compass, a map, and a list of French, German, and Spanish words.

Suddenly you hear voices. What language are they speaking? It's not French or German, and you're too far north for Spanish. You lay low, waiting. Finally a woman whispers in English, "Hello, pilot, we can help."

To trust the woman, turn to page **164**.

To stay hidden, turn to **165**.

You step out from behind the tree. "We are Dutch," the woman says. "We will help you find your way home." They take you to a farmhouse and show you the weapons they have gathered. "We fight the Germans any way we can," they tell you.

Two nights later, they take you to meet a French partisan group who guides you to Spain. From Spain, a neutral country, you fly to England. You fly many more missions before Germany surrenders on May 7, 1945. The war in Europe ends the next day. You return home to Canada as a hero.

To follow another path, turn to page 119.
To read the conclusion, turn to page 211.

Nazi soldiers were heavily armed.

You wait and listen. The voices fade away. Then you hear men speaking German. A man passes so close you can see the shine of his rifle in the moonlight. You don't dare breathe.

You wait several minutes. The voices move away, so you stand up. You find yourself looking directly into the face of a young German soldier. He seems as surprised as you are.

To stay where you are, turn to page **170**.

To run, turn to page **171**.

You jump out of the plane. Your white parachute is an easy target for German rifles. Bullets pierce your parachute, and you crash onto the beach. Pain shoots through your leg.

A medic rushes to your side. "Your leg is broken," he says.

You are brought to a hospital in England. As your leg heals, you are given light duty at the air base. You stay there until the war ends in 1945. You finish your military service and return home.

To follow another path, turn to page 119.
To read the conclusion, turn to page 211.

"It's not far to safety," you say. "I can do it." But the entire plane begins to shake. You're shaking too as you grip the control stick. You pray that you can keep the plane in the air until you reach the airstrip near the beach.

By some miracle, you reach the airstrip. You make a bumpy landing, but you are safe. Relieved, you stagger out of the cockpit.

When the ground crew checks the plane, they find several bullet holes in the blades of your propellers. As soon as your plane is repaired, you fly more missions over France.

Allied troops advance through northwestern Europe, reclaiming territory from the Germans. You fly ahead, bombing German tanks and artillery.

Turn the page.

As the Allies push farther inland, they reclaim an airstrip in France. It becomes your new base. From this airstrip, you fly missions into Germany, dropping bombs on German cities.

Many German cities, including Berlin, were destroyed by bombs during the war.

It's the most difficult thing you've ever done. You know your bombs may be killing German women and children. But you do it anyway. War is a terrible thing. The sooner it ends, the fewer lives that will be lost.

The Germans surrender on May 7, 1945. On May 8, the war in Europe officially ends. At long last, you return to Canada. You stay in the Air Force and train young pilots. You hope that they'll never have to fight another world war.

To follow another path, turn to page 119.
To read the conclusion, turn to page 211.

Seconds later, German soldiers surround you. They take you to a stalag in Germany. The prison camp is surrounded by barbed wire. German soldiers man the guard towers. Twice a day, they give you thin, tasteless soup and black bread. You struggle to keep warm in the freezing barracks.

You and the other prisoners try to make the best of a bad situation. When the weather is good, you play baseball in the yard.

You are finally released when the war ends in 1945. Getting home renews your health and your spirit.

To follow another path, turn to page 9.
To read the conclusion, turn to page 101.

You run and dodge. A bullet whizzes past you, but you keep going. The German shouts. He shoots again and misses. Maybe you have a chance. As you run, you look over your shoulder. Is he still behind you? No. But another German steps out of the woods and shoots you in the chest. You die in a farm field far from home.

THE END

To follow another path, turn to page 119.
To read the conclusion, turn to page 211.

It's only a short flight across the English Channel to your air base. At first, the Tiffie flies well, but then the shaking worsens. What's wrong? The engine sputters. You try to gain control, but the plane plunges into the sea. You die on impact.

THE END

To follow another path, turn to page 119.
To read the conclusion, turn to page 211.

You go to your friend's aid. You urge him to crawl back to the trench, but he dies in your arms. You have no choice but to leave him there. During a break in the shooting, you dash back to the trench. But you are not fast enough. An enemy bullet kills you before you reach safety.

THE END

To follow another path, turn to page 119.
To read the conclusion, turn to page 211.

Trying to escape would be suicide. You sign. So do the other officers.

You spend the next four years in one prison camp or another. One day, you see an American pilot flying overhead. He flies low, and you see him smile. He waves and drops a chocolate bar out the window. Other planes follow. One pilot drops out his shoes and shirt for you. What wonderful gifts!

The war is over! The Allies have won, and you'll be free soon. You can't wait to see Canada again.

THE END

To follow another path, turn to page 119.
To read the conclusion, turn to page 211.

You refuse to sign. Japanese guards tie you to a tree. For two days, they give you no food or water. "Sign!" they say, and you finally agree.

You are weak. The men in your hut insist that you go to the hospital. Thank goodness the camp hospital has remained open. The doctors and nurses who shipped over with you continue to do their work, even though they are prisoners too.

At the hospital, a kind and gentle nurse takes care of you. The two of you plan to marry when you get well. But you don't get well. You develop a fever and die in the hospital one year after you arrived in Hong Kong.

THE END

To follow another path, turn to page 119.
To read the conclusion, turn to page 211.

The United States entered war against Japan and Germany on December 8, 1941.

America Joins the Fight

On Sunday afternoon, December 7, 1941, you are reading a Superman comic book. The radio plays in the background. Suddenly the music stops.

"We interrupt this program to bring you a special news bulletin," a man says. "The Japanese have attacked Pearl Harbor, Hawaii, by air, President Franklin Roosevelt has just announced."

The next day, the U.S. Congress declares war on Japan. On December 9, you huddle close to the radio while President Roosevelt speaks to the nation.

Turn the page.

"We expect to eliminate the danger from Japan," he says. "But it would serve us ill if we accomplished that and found that the rest of the world was dominated by Hitler and Mussolini."

Suddenly everyone is talking about the war. At the movies, you watch newsreels about the fighting in Europe.

On November 11, 1942, Congress lowers the draft age from 21 to 18. "I'm joining the Navy as soon as I graduate from high school this spring," one of your friends says. "Why not join me?"

You were planning to begin college. Maybe this war will end before you are drafted.

To sign up for the Navy as soon as you graduate, go to page **179**.

To go to college, turn to page **184**.

You enlist in the Navy. "Do you want to be a medic?" an officer asks.

"Yes, sir," you answer. "I hope to be a doctor some day."

You go to Great Lakes Naval Base near Chicago for training. In basic training, you learn how to shoot a rifle and defend yourself.

Then you attend a special school to become a pharmacist's mate. This training allows you to perform first aid and nursing duties. When your training is complete, you report for duty.

"Take the train to San Diego," an officer tells you.

"Where am I going?" you ask.

"You'll know when you get there," an officer says. "In time of war, we keep information secret."

Turn the page.

In San Diego, you board an old luxury liner. The Navy is using the ship to carry soldiers to war. It is your first time on a boat, and you and everyone else are seasick. After a few days, you feel better. Many of the people on your boat are medics, nurses, or doctors. There is also a Marine division headed to battle. You enjoy beating the Marines at card games.

It takes nearly 30 days to reach the Solomon Islands in the South Pacific. You stop at Guadalcanal to drop off troops. You pick up more Marines and go to Choiseul Island. The Japanese occupy Choiseul.

On October 28, 1943, you watch as Marines land on Choiseul to attack the Japanese. The troops on your ship go ashore by boat. When they are wounded, you care for them. By the battle's end, 13 Marines and 143 Japanese soldiers are dead.

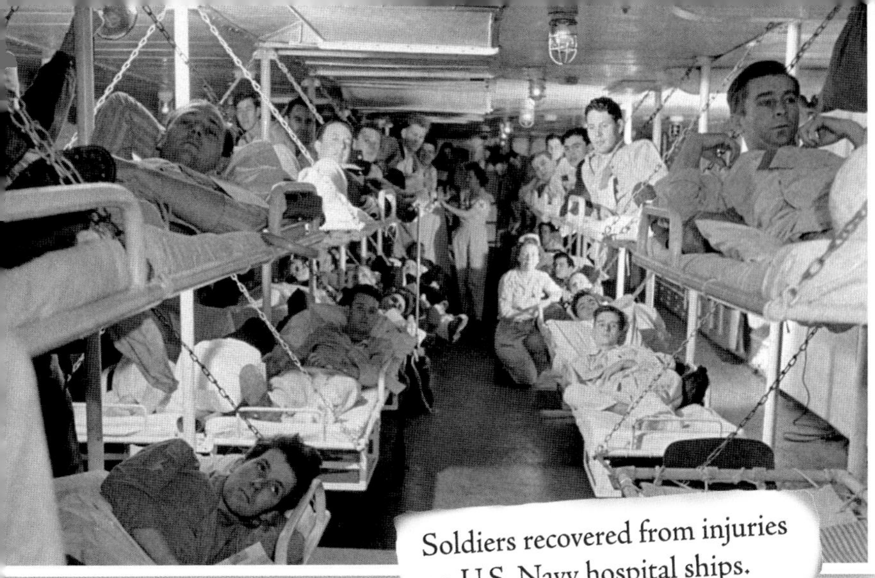

Soldiers recovered from injuries on U.S. Navy hospital ships.

A few months later, you transfer to a Navy hospital ship, the USS *Relief*. The ship, painted white with red crosses all along the side, is big enough to treat 1,000 wounded soldiers at a time. It carries 120 medical corpsmen like you, 20 doctors, and 12 Navy nurses.

Between battles, you prepare medicines, sharpen needles, and make bandages. During battles, you don't have time for anything except treating wounded soldiers.

Turn the page.

As the war continues, the ship goes wherever the Marines, Navy, or Army is fighting. The ship transports wounded soldiers and sailors to hospitals in Hawaii.

In January 1945, your ship is one of almost 900 ships headed for Iwo Jima. The island is only about 650 miles from Tokyo, Japan's largest city.

"We're taking more than 110,000 Marines to attack Japan," an officer says. "No foreign army has ever beaten the Japanese on their own territory. We'll be the first."

It takes 40 days to reach Iwo Jima. At 2:00 in the morning on February 19, Navy ships fire on Iwo Jima. An hour later, the smoke is so thick that it's hard to breathe. In the brief lull, American planes bomb the island.

U.S. troops used underwater vehicles to reach Iwo Jima's shore.

"I've counted more than 100 of our planes," another American soldier yells. "And more are coming." Once the planes fly over, the ships begin firing their big guns again.

At 8:30, your commander sends the landing force to shore. Some medics have to stay on the ship. Others will go with the landing force.

To go ashore, turn to page **191**.

To wait onboard the ship, turn to page **196**.

You graduate from high school in 1942 and take a summer job in a weapons factory. Many factories are helping with the war effort. In the fall, you begin college classes. But in November 1942, you are drafted into the U.S. Army.

You report to Fort Dix in New Jersey for two weeks of basic training. Then you go to Fort Bragg, North Carolina, where you train to be a cannoneer in a field artillery unit. You learn how to move, assemble, and fire a howitzer. It takes almost a dozen men to handle this huge gun.

Howitzers were large and powerful weapons.

On August 19, 1943, you board USS *Henry Gibbins*. You are so seasick that you can't eat. You want to sleep, but your bunk is tiny. Every time you roll over, you hit your head on the bunk above.

The trip seems to last forever. Finally on September 2, 1943, the ship pulls into port. "Where are we?" you ask.

"Oran. It's in Algeria," someone says.

"Algeria? That's in North Africa. Are we fighting here?"

"Not anymore. The British already won this battle before we could get here."

You spend several weeks waiting for orders. Meanwhile, you camp beneath the hot desert sun. Sandstorms bury your cooking gear, and you are always shaking sand out of your shoes.

Turn the page.

Finally the commanding officer calls you together. "We have our orders," he says. "We're going to Italy to fight the Germans."

Three Landing Ship Tanks (LSTs) carry you across the Mediterranean Sea to Italy. You join with the 194th Field Artillery Group of the Fifth Army.

"Bring on the war!" you yell, but what comes first is rain. Mud makes the going impossible. The big guns tip over and get stuck. You are so tired that you crawl under a canvas tarp and sleep in the mud.

You awake to German soldiers firing on you from the surrounding hills. You fire back. The gunfire is so constant and loud that your ears hurt. The air is smoky. A nearby tank blows up, hit by German missiles. Another tank blocks the road.

You fight until December 25. On Christmas Day, the Army supplies a special Christmas dinner, packages from home, and a shipment of rain boots. After one day of rest, it's back to war.

On March 23, 1943, you reach the coastal city of Anzio, Italy. The beach is full of American and British troops. The Germans are dug in on the hills above the beach. They fire 300-pound shells at you.

You dig bunkers, which are underground homes to sleep in at night. Some of the men name theirs. There's a "Holler Inn" and a "Foxhole Hotel." You call yours "Dew Drop Inn." Every morning around 4:00, German planes bomb the beach. You are always tired and ready to crawl into your bunker, out of harm's way.

Turn the page.

Soldiers ate in their bunkers during lulls in the fighting.

During a break one evening, a soldier from a nearby British camp invites you to play cards. You would enjoy a good game, but maybe you should sleep while you can.

*To play cards, go to page **189**.*

*To stay in camp to sleep, turn to page **202**.*

You head off to the British camp and join your friends in a game of poker.

You play for chocolate bars. Army chocolate bars are so hard you have to break them apart with the butt of your gun. You don't mind losing chocolate.

When you return to your bunker, your friends are digging into it.

"I know he's in there," one man says.

"Who's in there?" you ask.

Everyone turns to stare at you. "You. At least we thought you were. A German shell landed directly on your bunker. We were trying to save your sorry life."

"Thanks," you say. "I may have lost the card game, but that game saved my life."

Turn the page.

British, New Zealand, and American troops fight side by side. By June 1943, the fighting at Anzio ends. You join several soldiers in a visit to Rome. Some men attend church services. Others visit the Roman ruins. The vacation is too short.

You spend another three months in Italy chasing the Germans north. In September 1943, you drive an LST to Marseilles, France. A few days later, you reach the town of Saint Benoit. You find it demolished and abandoned. Is it really abandoned? Some of the men want to check buildings for food. "It might be booby-trapped," an officer says.

To stay with the main unit on the road, turn to page **199**.

To check the buildings, turn to page **201**.

You climb over the ship's side and down a rope ladder into a small boat that takes you to shore. As soon as you hit the beach, Japanese soldiers start shooting at you from holes dug in the sand.

"Help!" a Marine shouts. He has been hit, but his wound is not serious. You call it a happy wound because he'll recover in a few days.

You bandage the soldier's wound and take him to a waiting boat. The boat will take him back to the ship for treatment. If you go along, you'll escape the worst of the fighting. But if you stay on shore, you can help other wounded men.

To stay on shore, turn to page **192**.

To return to the hospital ship, turn to page **205**.

Medics tended to wounded soldiers at makeshift first aid stations on Iwo Jima.

You stay to help. Men are screaming in pain. You give first aid to several wounded soldiers. One man dies in your arms. Others are so badly injured that they will die soon. As you rush toward another fallen soldier, you feel a searing pain in your arm. You've been shot!

"Help!" you call. A medic comes to your aid. He gives you morphine for your pain. Then he helps you back to the hospital ship.

A doctor removes the bullet. With a few days of rest, you'll recover. Most others aren't so lucky. An officer tells you, "Our company started with 310 men. Only 50 of us made it back to the ship."

When you are well enough, you go on deck and see the American flag flying over Iwo Jima.

In August 1945, a U.S. aircraft drops an atomic bomb on the Japanese city of Hiroshima. President Harry S. Truman announces the news from the cruiser USS *Augusta* in the Atlantic Ocean. He says that the bomb was more than 2,000 times more powerful than the largest bomb used to date.

A few days later, another American plane drops an atomic bomb on the Japanese city of Nagasaki. Finally the Japanese agree to surrender.

Turn the page.

The war is over! The captain orders all the ship's lights turned on. When you look over the harbor, you see thousands of Allied ships, their lights burning bright. Then every ship in the harbor fires their guns into the sky. It looks like a Fourth of July fireworks show.

Japan officially surrenders during a ceremony aboard the USS *Missouri* on September 2, 1945. Representatives from all the Allied countries are there. General Douglas MacArthur gives a speech. His chief of staff, Lieutenant General Richard Sutherland, leads the ceremony. Fleet Admiral Chester Nimitz signs on behalf of the United States.

After the war, the Allies take control of Japan to change it to a democracy. MacArthur is named supreme commander for the Allied nations.

Soldiers and sailors crowded the deck of the USS *Missouri* to watch the Japanese surrender.

Your commander asks if you would like to go with MacArthur to Japan. "You're the only one in the unit who was wounded, so the honor is yours. It's not an order. It's an invitation."

To go directly home, turn to page **206**.

To go with MacArthur, turn to page **208**.

Pharmacists performed tests aboard U.S. Navy hospital ships.

"I'm more useful in the lab," you say, and it's true. There are blood tests to run and medicines to prepare.

Soon boatload after boatload of wounded American soldiers reach the hospital ship. The ward is full, and you are busy giving injections to wounded soldiers.

Thanks to the skillful doctors on the ship, many seriously wounded soldiers survive the Battle of Iwo Jima. Those who don't are buried at sea with a simple ceremony.

The ship takes several trips to Hawaii to deliver wounded soldiers to hospitals. Then it returns to battle. On April 1, 1945, when the ship is in Okinawa, Japanese planes attack. You are in the middle of a delicate test when the battle alarm sounds.

To go to your battle station, turn to page **198**.

To finish the test, turn to page **203**.

The test will have to wait. You run to your battle station. Once it is secured, you notice a plane going by, and then another. Two Japanese pilots fly their planes into the deck of the USS *South Dakota* nearby. Flames erupt, burning several soldiers. The ship's firefighters get control of the fire. The ship survives.

After the Battle of Okinawa ends, your ship goes to the Philippines. It picks up troops going to Japan for a planned invasion. But the invasion never comes. After American planes drop atomic bombs on two Japanese cities in August, Japan surrenders. At last, the war is over.

To follow another path, turn to page 119.
To read the conclusion, turn to page 211.

You stay on the road while others run toward the village. Suddenly you hear a large boom. "The town is booby-trapped!" an officer yells.

The Germans left traps as they retreated. Bombs explode as troops accidentally set them off.

One of your friends is buried beneath the rubble. "Help!" he screams. You dig through the rock until you find him. You carefully pull him out.

"Your leg is crushed," you say. "But you'll live." That was a close call. You hope this war ends soon before you lose any of your friends.

In December 1944, you reach Germany and cross the Rhine River. You continue to fight the German Army on their home soil. They seem as tired of war as you are.

Turn the page.

On May 7, 1945, Germany surrenders. The Allies declare May 8 as Victory in Europe (V-E) Day. The Germans have surrendered. The European part of the war is over.

You spend several weeks in Oberammergau, Germany, waiting for your official release papers. While you are waiting, you learn that the Germans killed millions of Jewish people.

"They set up concentration camps where they killed their Jewish neighbors," a soldier tells you. "We went into one of the camps. The people who were still alive were starving."

You've seen enough death to last a lifetime. You want to go home. But an officer asks if you will consider fighting in the Pacific.

To wait in Germany for your release papers, turn to page **206**.

To go to the Pacific to fight, turn to page **207**.

You go from one bombed-out building to another hoping to find something to eat. Then you hear a chicken cluck. A fresh egg would be a treat. As you step into the barn, your leg brushes against a wire.

BOOM! The barn was booby-trapped, and you've just set it off. You die instantly.

THE END

To follow another path, turn to page 119.
To read the conclusion, turn to page 211.

You're exhausted. Constant artillery fire keeps you up all night. So you crawl into your bunker and collapse on your cot. You are sleeping soundly when the Germans start firing.

A shell lands directly on your bunker. You're buried beneath the rubble. The men of your unit dig you out, but it is too late. You were killed instantly when the shell hit. The war is over for you.

THE END

To follow another path, turn to page 119.
To read the conclusion, turn to page 211.

About 50,000 Allied soldiers were killed or wounded in the Battle of Okinawa.

You finish up the test quickly. Meanwhile, American antiaircraft guns shoot a Japanese plane out of the sky. "We were lucky they were close by," you say to a friend.

The Battle of Okinawa is a bloody battle. For nearly three months, you work day and night treating injured soldiers.

When the battle ends in late June, more than 7,300 Americans have died. Another 32,000 are wounded. But the Japanese lost nearly 100,000 soldiers. It is a stunning defeat for the Japanese.

Turn the page.

In August, your ship heads for Japan. But on August 14, the captain makes an announcement. "We're going home. The war is over."

American planes dropped powerful atomic bombs on Japan. Thousands of Japanese people were killed. Japan's leader, Emperor Hirohito, agreed to surrender.

The ship turns around and brings soldiers back to the United States. You spend the journey treating seasick soldiers. When you reach California, you are discharged. Home at last, you're proud that you served your country.

To follow another path, turn to page 119.
To read the conclusion, turn to page 211.

There will be plenty for you to do on the ship. You help load the wounded men into the small boat for the trip back to the ship. As you are climbing into the boat, you feel a sudden pain in your chest. There's blood on your shirt.

"I've been shot!" you cry.

The wound is serious. The last sight you see is the red cross on the sleeve of a medic trying to stop the bleeding. You are one of 6,800 American soldiers who die on Iwo Jima.

THE END

To follow another path, turn to page 119.
To read the conclusion, turn to page 211.

U.S. soldiers returning from war were welcomed into New York Harbor.

It's time to go home. When your release papers arrive, you take a ship to New York. Then you catch the first train home. Mom and Dad throw a quiet celebration. You're just happy to have survived and to be with your family again.

THE END

To follow another path, turn to page 119.
To read the conclusion, turn to page 211.

You decide to sign up for service in the Pacific. In late July 1945, you reach Okinawa, an island off the coast of Japan. "We'll be invading Japan," your officer tells you.

But the invasion never comes. On August 6, 1945, the United States drops an atomic bomb on the Japanese city of Hiroshima. Three days later, the United States drops a bomb on the city of Nagasaki. Hundreds of thousands of Japanese people are injured or killed in both cities. Japanese Emperor Hirohito agrees to end the war.

On September 2, 1945, Japan officially surrenders. The war is over. You take the first available ship home and pray that there will never be another war.

To follow another path, turn to page 119.
To read the conclusion, turn to page 211.

It's an honor to join General MacArthur. You travel with MacArthur to Atsugi Air Base in Japan, between Yokohama and Tokyo.

General Douglas MacArthur commanded the occupation of Japan following the war.

One day, as you are returning to your barracks, you meet the general face-to-face. MacArthur is nearly 65 years old, but he's still strong and capable. You smile as you salute him.

After two weeks in Japan, you return by ship to San Diego. After finishing your military service, you follow your dream to become a doctor. You hope the world will never again go to war.

To follow another path, turn to page 119.
To read the conclusion, turn to page 211.

The fiery attack on Pearl Harbor on December 7, 1941, launched the United States into World War II.

World War II

World War II took place on two fronts, in Europe and in the Pacific. It began in 1939, when Germany invaded Poland. Then Germany took over Denmark, Belgium, the Netherlands, and Norway.

In the Pacific, the Japanese attacked China in 1931 and in 1937. In 1940, Japan formed an alliance with Germany and Italy.

The United States hoped to stay out of the war. But on December 7, 1941, Japanese planes attacked Pearl Harbor, Hawaii. The next day, President Roosevelt and Congress declared war on Japan. On December 11, Germany and Italy declared war on the United States.

The United States joined the side of the Allies. The Allies included Great Britain, France, the United States, Canada, and many other countries. During the war, 1.1 million Canadians served in the armed forces. More than 16 million men and women served in the U.S. military.

The Allied invasion of Normandy in France on June 6, 1944, was a turning point in the war. From that point, the Allies regained territory in Europe, pushing the German Army back to its homeland. The war in Europe officially ended on May 8, 1945.

Meanwhile, battles raged in the Pacific. Japan won the early battles. But in June 1942, the Allies won the Battle of Midway. It was the first definite Allied victory in the Pacific. After that, the Allies pounded the Japanese military. Still, Japan refused to surrender.

Then in August 1945, the United States dropped atomic bombs on the Japanese cities of Hiroshima and Nagasaki. Between 70,000 and 100,000 people were killed in Hiroshima. About 40,000 were killed or declared missing in Nagasaki. On August 14, 1945, the Japanese agreed to surrender. They signed the surrender documents September 2, 1945. The war was over.

The United States dropped atomic bombs on two Japanese cities to end World War II.

At the end of the war, Allied troops discovered concentration camps in Germany and Poland. Between 5 and 6 million Jewish men, women, and children died in these camps. The Nazis also killed many Polish Catholics, Jehovah's Witnesses, and disabled people. After the war, German leaders were put on trial for these war crimes.

Allied troops freed sick and starving men, women, and children from German concentration camps after the war.

No one knows the exact number of people killed in World War II. Experts guess that 17 million soldiers died in battle. Even more civilians died as a result of bombing raids, massacres, and war-related illnesses. Nearly 451,000 U.S. men and women died in service.

It took years for most European countries to recover from the war. Bombed cities in Japan suffered for years after the war, as did many island nations in the Pacific.

World War II killed more people than any war in world history. It also destroyed more property and changed more lives than any other war. People everywhere continue to hope that the world will never again fight another war.

Time Line

September 1931 — Japanese troops take over the state of Manchuria in China.

July 1937 — Chinese and Japanese troops clash near Beijing, China.

September 1, 1939 — Germany invades Poland.

September 3, 1939 — Great Britain, France, Australia, and New Zealand declare war on Germany.

September 10, 1939 — Canada declares war on Germany.

April 9, 1940 — Germany invades Norway and Denmark.

May 10, 1940 — Germany invades France, the Netherlands, Belgium, and Luxembourg.

June 10, 1940 — Italy declares war on Great Britain and France.

June 14, 1940 — German troops enter Paris, France.

July 10, 1940 — Battle of Britain begins.

September 27, 1940 — Germany, Italy, and Japan unite as the Axis powers.

May 1941 — Germany stops bombing Great Britain, ending the Battle of Britain.

December 7, 1941 — Japan bombs Pearl Harbor, Hawaii.

December 8, 1941 — The United States, Canada, and Great Britain declare war on Japan.

December 11, 1941 — Germany and Italy declare war on the United States.

December 25, 1941 — Hong Kong surrenders to the Japanese.

September 3, 1943 — Italy surrenders to the Allies.

June 6, 1944 — Allies stage D-Day invasion of Normandy in France.

February 19, 1945 — U.S. forces land on Iwo Jima, off the coast of Japan.

April 1, 1945 — U.S. forces invade the Japanese island of Okinawa.

May 7, 1945 — Germany surrenders to the Allies.

May 8, 1945 — The war in Europe officially ends. This day becomes known as V-E (Victory in Europe) Day.

August 6, 1945 — The United States drops an atomic bomb on Hiroshima, Japan.

August 9, 1945 — The United States drops an atomic bomb on Nagasaki, Japan.

September 2, 1945 — Japan signs surrender papers. World War II is over.

Other Paths to Explore

In this book, you've seen how the events experienced during World War II look different from three points of view.

Perspectives on history are as varied as the people who lived it. You can explore other paths on your own to learn more about what happened. Seeing history from many points of view is an important part of understanding it.

Here are some ideas for other World War II points of view to explore:

- Many European Jews went into hiding to avoid the Nazis. What would it have been like to spend two or three years hiding in a small French town or on a Dutch farm?

- Life at home in Canada or the United States was not easy during the war. Brothers, husbands, and fathers were away serving in the military. What would life have been like for families waiting at home?

- Germany was considered the enemy of the United States. However, many Germans arrived in North America during the years before the war. What was life like for them?

World War II on the Home Front:

An Interactive History Adventure

By Martin Gitlin

Consultant:
Timothy Solie
Adjunct Professor
Department of History
Minnesota State University, Mankato

Table of Contents

About Your Adventure

YOU are living in the United States in the early 1940s. The world is at war. How will you help your country fight for its freedom?

In this book you'll explore how the choices people made meant the difference between life and death. The events you'll experience happened to real people.

Chapter One sets the scene. Then you choose which path to read. Follow the directions at the bottom of each page. The choices you make will change your outcome. After you finish one path, go back and read the others for new perspectives and more adventures.

YOU CHOOSE the path you take through history.

Adolf Hitler, the leader of Germany and the Nazi Party, stirred up hatred of Jews.

CHAPTER 1

THE COMING OF WAR

The guns fell silent in 1918. World War I was over. Many called it "the war to end all wars" because they believed such a terrible conflict could never happen again. But they were wrong. Only 21 years later, war would again engulf the world.

Dictator Adolf Hitler and the Nazi political party took control of Germany in the early 1930s. The country had fallen into a deep economic depression. Hitler targeted the Jewish people, whom he blamed for Germany's economic problems. He also blamed German misery on the 1919 Treaty of Versailles that had followed the fighting. It had punished Germany for starting World War I. It also forced Germany's government to pay billions of dollars to its European neighbors.

Turn the page.

Meanwhile, storm clouds gathered over Asia. Japan had invaded China. Many Americans were alarmed by the events in Europe and Asia. But they had big problems at home. The Great Depression that began in 1929 left about 25 percent of Americans unemployed. Millions were poor, and many were homeless. Americans were too concerned about finding their next meal to worry about a potential war thousands of miles away.

That potential war in Europe became a terrible reality when Germany invaded Poland on September 1, 1939. Soon Great Britain and France declared war on Germany. But few could have imagined how powerful a military the Germans had developed. Germany quickly conquered Poland and several other countries. The world was shocked when the Germans took over France in just six weeks.

A woman couldn't hide her misery as she dutifully saluted the invading German Nazis.

Some Americans believed the United States should enter the war. But many Americans were isolationists who felt that their country should stay out.

Turn the page.

Everything changed December 7, 1941. That morning hundreds of Japanese planes attacked and destroyed a U.S. naval base at Pearl Harbor in Hawaii. More than 2,000 Americans were killed.

The United States entered World War II after the 1941 attack on Pearl Harbor.

Congress quickly declared war on Japan. A few days later the United States was at war with Germany as well.

The battle lines had been drawn. Germany, Italy, and Japan had formed an alliance called the Axis. The United States joined the Soviet Union, Britain, and other nations to form what was known as the Allies.

Men and women from all over the United States signed up immediately to join the war effort. Millions of men were drafted to fight and sent overseas. But the war didn't just affect the new soldiers. It changed the lives of all Americans.

To be a woman married to an American soldier fighting overseas, turn to page **231**.

To be a 12-year-old boy in San Diego, turn to page **265**.

To be a wounded black war veteran from the segregated South, turn to page **291**.

Average net paid circulation for November exceeded
Daily---1,925,000
Sunday-3,750,000

DAILY NEWS

Copr. 1941 by News Syndicate Co. Inc. NEW YORK'S PICTURE NEWSPAPER Trade Mark Reg. U. S. Pat. Off.

Vol. 23. No. 142 | New York, Monday, December 8, 1941★ | 64 Main + 4 Manhattan Pages | 2 Cents IN CITY LIMITS

JAPAN A
WAR
WITH U.S

Hawaii, Philippines
And Guam Bombe

FLEET HITS BAC

CHAPTER 2

TO WORK OR NOT TO WORK

It's a relaxing afternoon in December 1941. You're with your husband, Edward, and a few of your friends in your New York City apartment. Soft music is playing on the radio, but nobody is paying attention to it.

Suddenly, everyone is quiet. A news report has interrupted the music.

"We have witnessed this morning the attack of Pearl Harbor and a severe bombing of Pearl Harbor by army planes, undoubtedly Japanese," states the announcer. "It's no joke. It's a real war."

Turn the page.

President Roosevelt spoke to Congress the day after the attack.

You've never even heard of Pearl Harbor, but you know this indeed means war. The party is over.

The next day you listen to President Franklin D. Roosevelt on your radio. He calls December 7 "a date which will live in infamy." The United States is at war with Japan.

You stare at Edward. He says nothing, but you know what he's thinking. You know he's going to join the fight. You just don't know when.

The following day you find out. Edward packs his bags and enlists in the Navy. You don't know if you will ever see your beloved husband again. Will your 9-year-old daughter, Elizabeth, grow up without a father?

You are feeling lonely and afraid. Should you stay in New York and find a job? Or should you join your wealthy mother in Virginia? You can stay at her home without having to work. But you also want to do your part for the war effort.

To find a job, turn to page **234**.

To move to Virginia, turn to page **236**.

You're like most married women of the time. You have grown used to cooking, cleaning, and taking care of your family. Edward made a fine living in advertising. But now his large income is gone. You need money to pay for food and rent.

One day your friend Edna tells you that a local steel plant has been converted to a factory. It produces fighter planes and other aircraft. They're looking for female workers to replace the men who have become soldiers.

"When are you going over there?" you ask.

"Right now," she answers. "Do you want to come?" The need is so great that you are hired after a 10-minute interview. Soon you are operating heavy equipment that makes sheet metal for planes.

After an eight-hour day on the job, your muscles are aching and you are exhausted. But you are proud of your work.

You realize that you are capable of being more than a mother and housewife. You are just as productive on the job as the men. But then you discover something. The men make more money than the women!

You tell Edna that you're going to complain to the boss, but she warns you to keep quiet. You realize it probably won't help to gripe, but you feel it's a matter of right and wrong. On the other hand, you don't want to lose your job.

→*To keep quiet even though you're mad, turn to page* **237**.

→*To complain to the boss, turn to page* **247**.

The first few months in Virginia are ideal. But you begin to question your decision to stay at home with Elizabeth and your mother. You ask yourself, "What are you doing to help the war effort?" Your answer? "Nothing."

You think back to the flying lessons you took in college. You also recall reading an article in the newspaper about women flying planes from factories to military bases. Other women are testing rebuilt planes. You consider becoming a test pilot.

You can also do more right here in Virginia. You could volunteer to help the soldiers and the war effort.

To stay in Virginia and do volunteer work, turn to page **240**.

To become a test pilot, turn to page **244**.

"Rosie the Riveter" came to symbolize the many women who worked during the war.

You hate to hold in your anger about a man earning more money than you. But you need the steady income. And helping the war effort makes you feel good about yourself.

Turn the page.

When summer rolls around, you have a problem. Elizabeth is home from school and you have no one to watch her.

You place an ad for a babysitter in the local grocery store. Several teenage girls stop by your home to be interviewed. But none of them seem right.

Now what? You must ensure Elizabeth's safety, but you can't quit your job. You're thinking about taking in a trustworthy boarder who can live in your house and pay rent. You also have a chance to take the "graveyard shift" at work. That would allow you to work nights while your daughter is sleeping and be with her during the day.

To bring in a boarder, turn to page **242**.

To take the graveyard shift, turn to page **246**.

OUR HOME FRONT
IS THE
PRODUCTION FRONT
FOR VICTORY
BUY
Buy War Savings Bonds Now! THROUGH
YOUR COMPANY'S VOLUNTARY PAYMENT PLAN
VICTORY LEGION
CARNEGIE - ILLINOIS
PRODUCTION DRIVE COMMITTEE

You are tempted to travel to Texas for training as a test pilot. But you can't leave Elizabeth. Her father is already gone and may not come back. She can't lose her mother too.

But you know you must do something to contribute to the war effort. You hear that volunteers are needed at a canteen. When you stop by, the woman in charge explains what it's all about.

"This is where soldiers on leave from the war and others who are heading overseas come for entertainment, food, and drinks," she says. "We serve doughnuts and coffee and we host a dance once a month. We can sure use your help."

"I'd like that," you say enthusiastically.

Soldiers and sailors enjoyed the entertainment at a San Diego canteen in 1942.

You are not so sure you like it after a few minutes during your first shift. You hear angry words being exchanged between a sailor and a woman. Should you get in the middle of the argument or should you let them work it out for themselves?

To try to ignore it, turn to page **258.**

To get involved, turn to page **263.**

You're speaking with possible boarders and a woman named Gloria has brought you to tears.

"We were destroyed by the Depression," she says. "We had no money. And just when my husband found a job, he was drafted into the Army. He was shot and died three months ago."

Gloria begs you to allow her to stay with you even though she can't pay rent. She promises to take care of Elizabeth and do the cooking and cleaning. You can't say no.

Elizabeth couldn't be happier. She smiles as she talks about all the games she and Gloria play. She adds that Gloria has a nice boyfriend who stops by and that the two spend a lot of time in the basement.

You wonder why Gloria would have a boyfriend just a few months after her husband was killed. You become suspicious. You search the basement and find a large bundle hidden behind your sewing machine. It's wrapped in cloth that matches one of Gloria's dresses. You open the bundle. And to your shock, it's full of money!

You are tempted to use the money to pay bills, but you fear big trouble if you do. Maybe you should go to the police.

To go to the police, turn to page **250**.

To take the money, turn to page **262**.

It's August 1943. You hear from a college friend that the newly formed Women Airforce Service Pilots (WASP) is looking for female aviators for training. You have a pilot's license and flight experience. Perfect!

You leave Elizabeth in your mother's care and are accepted as a trainee in Sweetwater, Texas. When you arrive you speak to Jackie Cochran, the director of the WASP program. You admire Cochran, one of the greatest pilots in American history. She even set a national air speed record, flying from New York to Miami in just over four hours.

Cochran has words of warning for you. "This could be dangerous," she says. "You will be testing warplanes. They might not all be safe. But we must find out. Your mission is important for the safety of our bombers overseas."

Your first two missions go well. But on your third mission, the unthinkable happens.

Jackie Cochran (right) was a top racing pilot.

You're flying a twin-engine plane when you notice you are running out of fuel. The fuel gauge must be broken! You are flying over an area with many houses. You can try to bring the plane down, but you could land on a home and kill its residents. Or you can keep flying and hope to find an open area.

To keep flying, turn to page **255.**

To bring the plane down, turn to page **260.**

You never have liked the dark. But you have to overcome your fear and take the graveyard shift at the airplane factory. You need the job and your country needs workers.

It is often pitch black outside when you walk to work at midnight. No lights are allowed during air raid drills along the Atlantic coast. People are worried about a possible German attack on New York. Any lights that can be seen from warplanes would make a tempting target.

One night before you leave home you hear the sirens roaring. It's an air raid drill! Elizabeth is scared. You don't know if you should stay home with her and risk losing your job or go to work.

To stay home, turn to page **252**.

To go to work, turn to page **256**.

You have never been one to keep quiet when someone is taking advantage of you.

"Hey, Mr. Foster!" you greet your boss angrily. "Why am I making less money than the man I'm working with? I've been working here longer than he has and I do just as good a job."

"That's easy," he says. "You can't be doing as good a job. You're a woman. Women are weaker. This is hard, physical work."

"That's not true!" you yell. "I'm doing the same job just as well as any man here, and I should be paid the same!"

"How would you like to get paid nothing for having no job?" he asks.

Turn the page.

Men and women worked together to build planes for the war effort.

He's threatening to fire you. "I'd rather get paid nothing than work here," you tell Mr. Foster. "Either I get equal pay for equal work or I quit!"

"You won't have to quit," he answers. "You're fired!"

You storm out of the factory and walk home. You need money and now you have no job. You want to help the war effort and now you can't.

But you know that with so many men overseas there is a need for female workers. You start to feel better when you realize that other jobs are waiting for you. And you hope you'll be paid fairly.

THE END

To follow another path, turn to page 229.
To read the conclusion, turn to page 321.

You run to the police station and show an officer the cash.

"This money isn't stolen," says the officer. You are relieved, but only briefly. "It's counterfeit!" he says. "Phony money. Your boarder is a crook!"

You try to keep calm. The woman living in your house and her boyfriend are criminals. There was no dead husband. You're sure of it! She must have made up the entire story. And she's been spending every day with your daughter.

Soon the police raid your home. They arrest Gloria and her boyfriend.

The babysitter didn't work out. The boarder certainly didn't work out. You need the money, but keeping Elizabeth safe is more important. So you quit your job at the airplane factory and take another one as a waitress in a coffee shop. The owner lets Elizabeth stay with you until she returns to school.

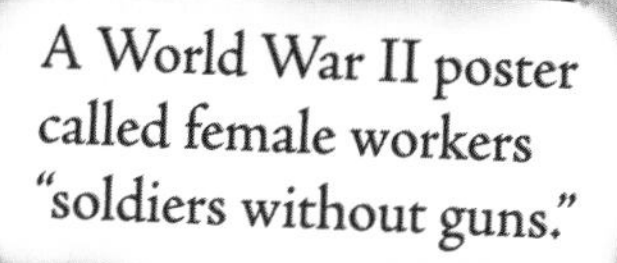

A World War II poster called female workers "soldiers without guns."

You are not earning as much money, but it's worth it. For the first time in a long time, you have peace of mind.

THE END

To follow another path, turn to page 229.
To read the conclusion, turn to page 321.

The air raid siren is wailing. Elizabeth is shaking, and you are hugging her.

"I know it's a little frightening," you whisper in her ear. "You'll be fine. I have to go to work now."

"No, no, no!" Elizabeth screams as she bursts into tears. "Don't go, mommy!"

You think for a moment. You've never missed work. You figure one night won't hurt. You call your boss. You don't want to lie and tell him you're sick, so you tell him the truth.

"Every child in this city is scared right now," he bellows. "You get yourself into work or don't bother coming in again!"

You have no choice. You know what is more important—and it's not your job. After you calmly tell your boss you won't be in tonight, he slams down the phone.

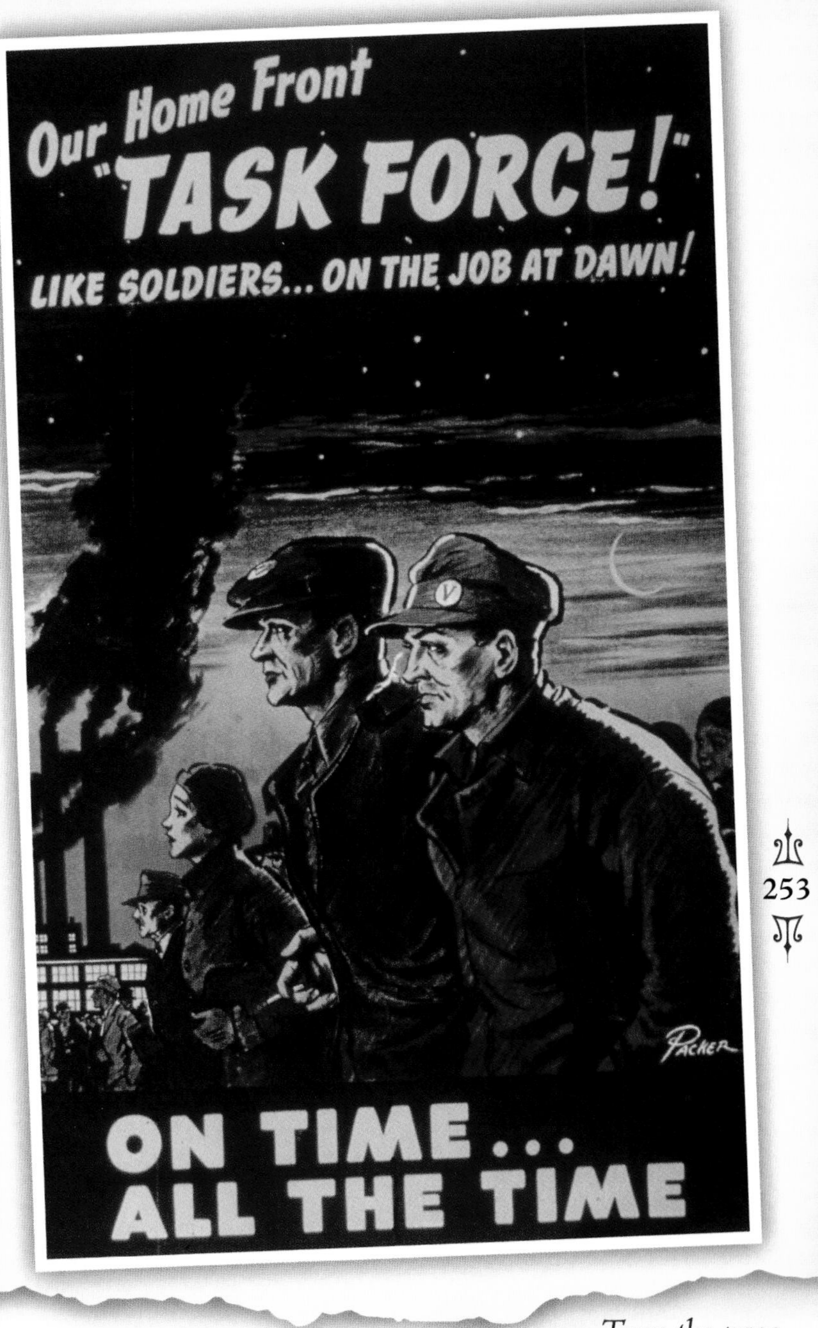

Turn the page.

You'll stay home but you know you must have a serious talk with Elizabeth. You put your arm around her and speak softly.

"During the Depression, people were out of work," you tell her. "People were poor. Some people were homeless. But President Roosevelt told Americans something that made them feel strong. He said, 'The only thing we have to fear is fear itself.' That means you have nothing to be afraid of but being afraid. And that's what I want you to think about."

Elizabeth says nothing, but you can tell she's taking it to heart. You know she'll be fine.

But will you? You'll have to start looking for a new job tomorrow. But as you face your uncertain future, you know you made the right choice.

THE END

To follow another path, turn to page 229.
To read the conclusion, turn to page 321.

You sweat and tremble. You can't find anywhere to land your plane. You are over a crowded city. But you don't panic. You are thinking more clearly than you ever have before.

You hope you have enough fuel to get away from the heart of the city. You keep flying at a steady clip. Even a crash landing on water could save your life. As soon as you find even the smallest open spot, you will try to land safely.

Suddenly, all your hopes are dashed. The plane begins diving to the earth. You know you're going to die. You think about how odd it is that you will die in the war without leaving the United States. Tears well up in your eyes as you realize you'll never see Edward or Elizabeth again. Then everything goes black.

THE END

To follow another path, turn to page 229.
To read the conclusion, turn to page 321.

You comfort Elizabeth as best you can. You have agreed to take the graveyard shift and you are stuck with it.

You also have other worries. Shortages of food and household goods are making it hard to shop. Sometimes you must visit several stores to find what you need. Meat, sugar, paper products, and rubber goods are especially hard to find because they're needed in the war effort.

You receive ration stamps that can be used to buy certain items. You spend hours trying to figure out what to buy and what stamps to keep for later use.

You want to make Elizabeth a special cake for her birthday, but it calls for butter. You have ration stamps, but there's no butter to be found.

Items were in short supply during the war, and shoppers had to use ration books.

Poor Elizabeth. There will be no special cake this year. You know she'll understand. You've talked about the many children suffering in Europe. Going without cake is nothing compared with their ordeal.

Despite problems shopping, you feel you are in control of your life. But there is one thing that is out of your control. You have no idea if Edward will come home alive. All you can do is hope and pray.

THE END

To follow another path, turn to page 229.
To read the conclusion, turn to page 321.

You are trying to ignore the argument between the woman and the sailor. And you're doing fine—for a while. But suddenly you hear a loud slap. Now you have to get involved.

"He wouldn't leave me alone, so I had to slap him," the woman says.

"All I wanted was a little kiss," the sailor replies.

You are angry. You stand face-to-face with the sailor.

"You are a disgrace to that Navy uniform!" you tell him. "What do you have to say for yourself?"

You are surprised when he starts to cry.

"I'm just scared," he says through his tears. "I'm shipping out in two days. I'm afraid of getting killed."

You are no longer mad. You put your arm around the sailor.

"This is a frightening time for everyone," you say softly. "You shouldn't be ashamed of being scared. Our greatest American heroes were scared. But you can't go around bothering women. Do you understand?"

"Yes, I do," he replies. "Thank you for understanding, ma'am."

The sailor sits down quietly and appears to be in deep thought. You know you got through to him. In some small way, you feel as if you have helped the war effort. And that makes you proud.

THE END

To follow another path, turn to page 229.
To read the conclusion, turn to page 321.

You are desperate. Everywhere you look below there are houses. But you know that you could run out of fuel at any second.

Suddenly you notice a large open field. This could be your only chance to land your plane safely. It's a tricky landing. If you pull up too short, you will crash through the roof of a house. If you fly too far, you will put your plane onto a busy street.

You are coming in too fast! You fear for your life. You finally slow the plane, but you're headed for a big yellow house. You miss the house by about 100 feet and land the plane safely at the edge of the field.

Women Airforce Service Pilots were based and trained in Sweetwater, Texas.

You know as you stumble from the cockpit that your days as a test pilot are over. You can't take any more chances. The boys overseas are risking their lives, but you have a daughter to take care of here at home. You can't afford to be killed.

THE END

To follow another path, turn to page 229.
To read the conclusion, turn to page 321.

You grab a handful of money from the bundle and count it. It's more than $2,000!

You head for the bank to deposit the cash. No more money worries for you! But suddenly your mind starts racing. What if the money was stolen? What if Gloria is keeping the money safe for a relative? You might get arrested for theft! You sure couldn't take care of Elizabeth if you were in jail!

You stop right then and race back home. You put the money back into the cloth bundle. You know in your heart that you did the right thing. Greed nearly got the better of you. You vow that won't happen again.

THE END

To follow another path, turn to page 229.
To read the conclusion, turn to page 321.

You have the unruly sailor escorted from the canteen.

"Are you all right?" you ask the woman.

"I'm fine," she says. "But I'm never coming here again."

"Oh, please do!" you reply. "Most of the men here are very nice and respectful. I urge you to stay. They have either been fighting the war or they will be soon. They need a friendly face and a friendly voice."

She agrees. Within minutes she is talking quietly with a soldier. You are thrilled to see both of them smiling.

THE END

To follow another path, turn to page 229.
To read the conclusion, turn to page 321.

The Japanese attack on Pearl Harbor prompted hatred of Japanese-Americans.

FIGHTING A WAR IN SAN DIEGO

You're sitting in the school lunchroom eating a peanut butter and jelly sandwich. Suddenly, your friend Tommy leans over and whispers in your ear.

"We're beating up Toki Yakimura after school," he says. "Pass the word."

"But he's a nice kid," you reply.

"We're beating him because he's a dirty Jap," Tommy says. "The Japanese attacked Pearl Harbor, and we're going to attack Toki with our fists."

Turn the page.

You don't understand. Toki is one of your best friends. He was born right here in San Diego. His parents own a grocery store. You always thought of the whole family as American. You often see their American flag flying in their front yard. And even if Toki is Japanese, what did he have to do with Pearl Harbor?

A Japanese-American shop owner erected a sign the day after Pearl Harbor.

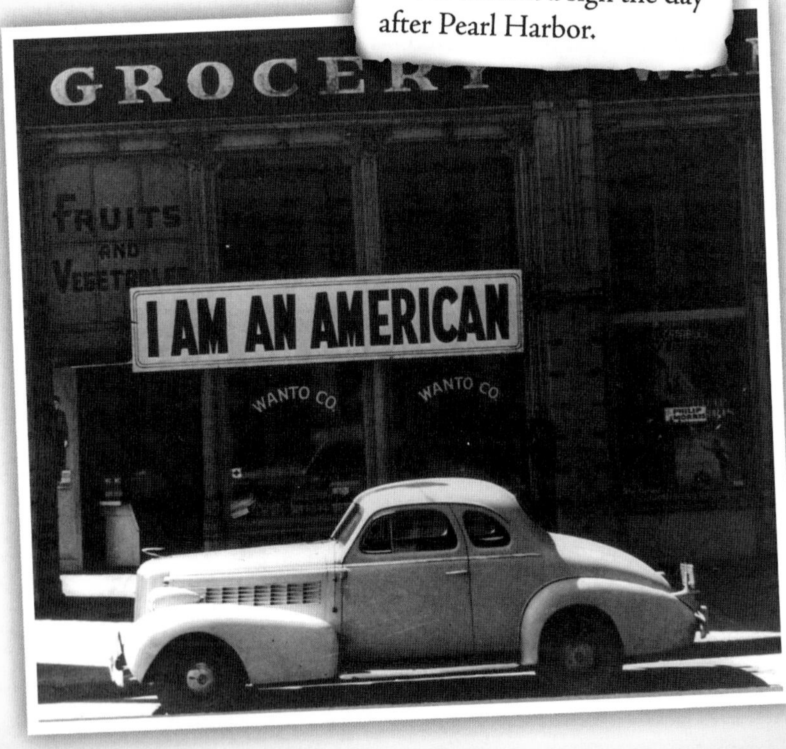

The school bell rings. You see Toki walking quickly out of the classroom. Tommy is one of five boys walking right behind him. They begin chasing Toki. And you begin chasing them. Soon Toki is surrounded. He looks frightened.

"Why are you doing this?" you yell. "Don't touch Toki!"

"You're either going to help us beat up Toki or you're a traitor," Tommy says. "And we hate traitors."

You would never join the attack, but do you risk losing your friends to defend Toki? If you try to save him, the boys might beat you up as well.

To run away, turn to page **268.**

To defend Toki, turn to page **274.**

You're scared. Your friends begin to punch Toki, who can't defend himself against five boys. But you can't fight that many classmates either.

"Help me!" Toki yells to you.

"No!" you scream back. And you run away.

You feel horrible as you race home. You are angry with yourself for not helping Toki. You tell your father about the fight.

"Do you know what's going on in Germany and the rest of Europe right now?" he asks.

You wonder why he's talking about Europe. Toki is Japanese.

"In Europe the Nazis are doing the same things to Jews like us that your friends did to Toki today. They are beating them up. They are even killing them. Nobody should allow what happened to Toki. But as a Jewish boy, you should understand that even more."

You know your father is right. You vow to be nice to Toki, but you feel too ashamed to apologize. Weeks go by. In late February 1942, you visit Toki at his house. He answers the door and the words pour out of you.

"I'm sorry I didn't help you that day," you tell him. "You were always my friend, Toki. And I want you to keep being my friend."

Jewish families faced near certain death after they surrendered to Nazi soldiers.

Turn the page.

Toki accepts your apology but he has sad news. "We're moving away," he says.

"Oh no!" you say. "I hope it's not because everyone has been so mean to you."

"That's not it," he answers. "We don't want to move. The government is making us move. They're moving all Japanese-Americans in the western United States to internment camps. I guess everyone is afraid of us."

"Don't worry, Toki," you blurt out without thinking. "I'll hide you. Meet me behind my house at 8 o'clock tonight. I won't let them take you away."

To hide Toki, go to page **271**.

To think over your options, turn to page **281**.

That night you look to your left, then to your right. You make sure your parents can't see you out the window of your house.

"Quick, follow me!" you whisper to Toki.

He is right behind you. You open the door to the shed next to the garage. He follows you inside.

"You'll be safe here," you tell him. "Nobody is taking my friend to some stupid camp. I'm going to sneak food and a blanket out to you."

You walk back into your house and open the refrigerator. You grab an apple for Toki and start out the door. But you hear a familiar voice.

"Where are you going?" It's your father.

"I'm going to eat this apple out back," you reply nervously.

Turn the page.

Just then you hear a knock on the front door. You follow your father as he walks over to answer it. Much to your shock, you see that it's Toki's parents. They are in a panic.

"Do you know where Toki is?" his mother asks you.

You thought you could lie, but one look at Toki's mother changes your mind. She is so upset that she's shaking. "I'm hiding Toki in the shed out back," you tell her. "And I want to hide you and Mr. Yakimura too."

"That's so kind," says Toki's mother. "Your heart is in the right place. But we would all get into much trouble if you did that."

Soon Toki and his family are out of your house. Three days later they're out of your neighborhood. But before they leave, you talk one more time with Toki.

"Will you see us off at the train station?" he asks. "It would mean a lot to me."

"Sure!" you answer. "It's the least I can do for my best friend."

You weren't just being nice. You feel now that Toki is your best friend. But when you tell your father about Toki's invitation, he suggests you stay home where it's safe.

"There could be trouble at the station," he says. "Some people might show up to yell bad things to the Japanese families leaving for internment camps. I don't want you to experience that kind of hatred."

➻*To meet Toki at the train station, turn to page* **276.**

➻*To stay away from the train station, turn to page* **278.**

"Don't let them do this!" Toki yells out to you. He is being hit by five of your classmates. He is not hitting back. He is just covering up his face.

"Lousy Jap!" says one boy as he slugs Toki in the stomach.

You rush in and grab Toki by the arm. You push Tommy back and run away with Toki. You're both faster than the others. They chase you but give up.

"You're a traitor!" Tommy screams at you. "You're no friend of mine!"

That evening you tell your father what happened. You both visit the parents of the boys who beat up Toki. Most of them promise they will punish their kids for the attack, but not Tommy's father.

"I was the one who told Tommy to teach that kid a lesson," he says. "The Jap families here are going to help the people in Japan attack San Diego. You watch and see."

When you return home you receive a phone call from Charlie, one of your classmates who had been hitting Toki that afternoon.

"There is only one way we can stay friends now after you saved that kid," he says. "You have to prove your loyalty to the United States by destroying something Japanese. Be in the woods after school tomorrow."

The only Japanese things you can think of are your Mom's good dishes. You want your friends back, but you don't want to destroy her Noritake china.

*To prove your loyalty in another way, turn to page **284**.*

*To join your friends in the woods, turn to page **288**.*

A small crowd has gathered at the station. You see hundreds of Japanese-Americans hauling anything they can carry on wheels or on their backs. Among them are the Yakimuras.

You have time to say a quick good-bye before you hear something that makes you mad.

"Good riddance, Japs!" screams a man in the crowd. "Don't come back!" shouts another. "This is for Pearl Harbor!" bellows an old woman.

You can't help yourself. "Hey! Shut up!" you yell. "Those are my friends!"

Suddenly you are surrounded. Every face looks angry. "Your friends, huh?" says a young man. "Maybe you should go with them! We're going to give you 10 seconds to get out of here."

Japanese-Americans were moved by train to internment camps in California and other states.

You have no choice. Everyone is bigger, stronger, and older than you are. You walk away, but you feel good about yourself. You stuck up for Toki and his family and you showed some courage.

THE END

To follow another path, turn to page 229.
To read the conclusion, turn to page 321.

Toki is not in school, of course. You thought you were the only kid who knew why. "Toki and his family are leaving for the internment camp," you tell your classmates. "It makes me sad."

"I'm sure not sad," Tommy says. "My father is planning a special surprise party for them."

"What do you mean?" you ask Tommy angrily. "What are you planning?"

"Let's just say the Yakimuras will know how we feel about the Japs when they're getting on that train," Tommy says. "My dad and I even bought some eggs and tomatoes to throw at them."

You wish you could be at the station. But your dad really didn't want you to go. You have to wait until school the next day to find out what happened. You decide that if Tommy had a surprise for Toki, you would have a surprise for Tommy.

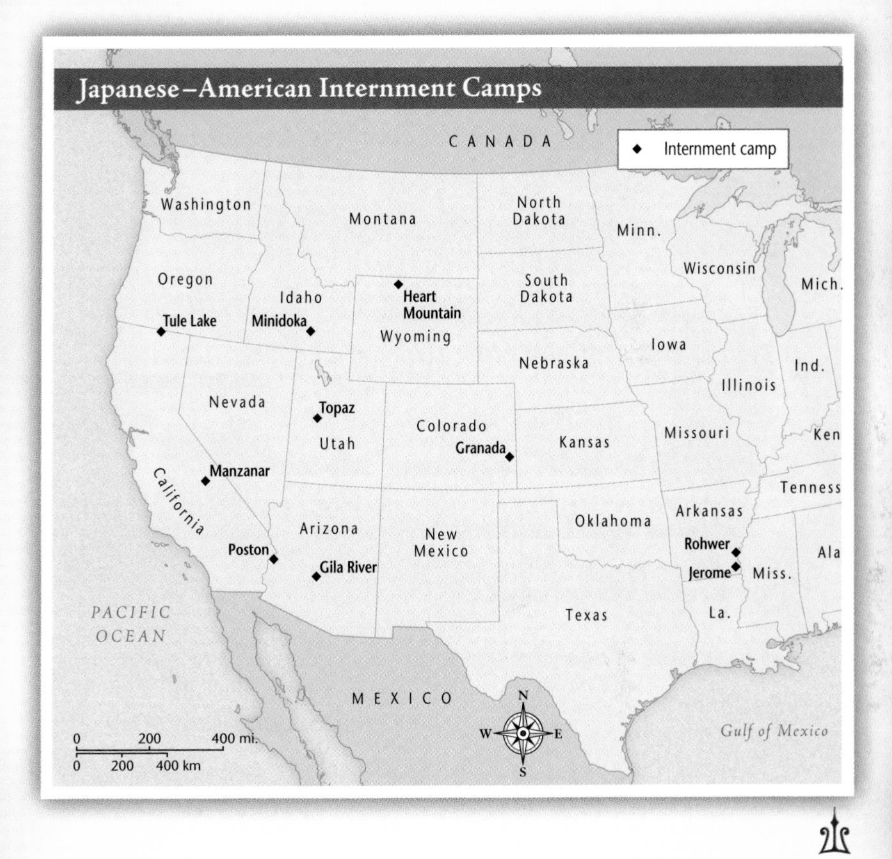

As soon as Tommy enters the classroom, he makes an announcement to the class. "I hit Toki with a tomato just before he got on the train!" he says with a laugh.

Turn the page.

But you're ready to get revenge for Toki. You brought a tomato to school. At recess you pull it out and rub it in Tommy's face.

"That's for Toki!" you yell.

Tommy jumps on you and you start fighting in the mud. Your teacher, Mrs. Stone, pulls you apart.

"What happened to you two?" she asks. "You used to be best friends."

"Not anymore," you reply. "And not ever again."

You have mud and tomato all over you. But you've never felt so proud. Toki will never know it, but you defended his honor.

THE END

To follow another path, turn to page 229.
To read the conclusion, turn to page 321.

You've been having doubts about your plan to hide Toki. But you are surprised when he comes to the front door of your house.

"Why aren't you hiding?" you ask.

"I have to be with my family," says Toki. "We always stick together." As he slowly turns to leave, you realize your plan wouldn't have worked. But you feel so sad.

You are sitting in your bedroom with your head in your hands. Your father comes in. "What's wrong?" he asks. You explain your plan to him.

He agrees that your plan wouldn't work. "But I'm proud of you," he says. "It showed that you have feelings for other people."

"But Dad," you reply, "if we as a Jewish family were in Germany right now, wouldn't you want someone to hide us?"

Turn the page.

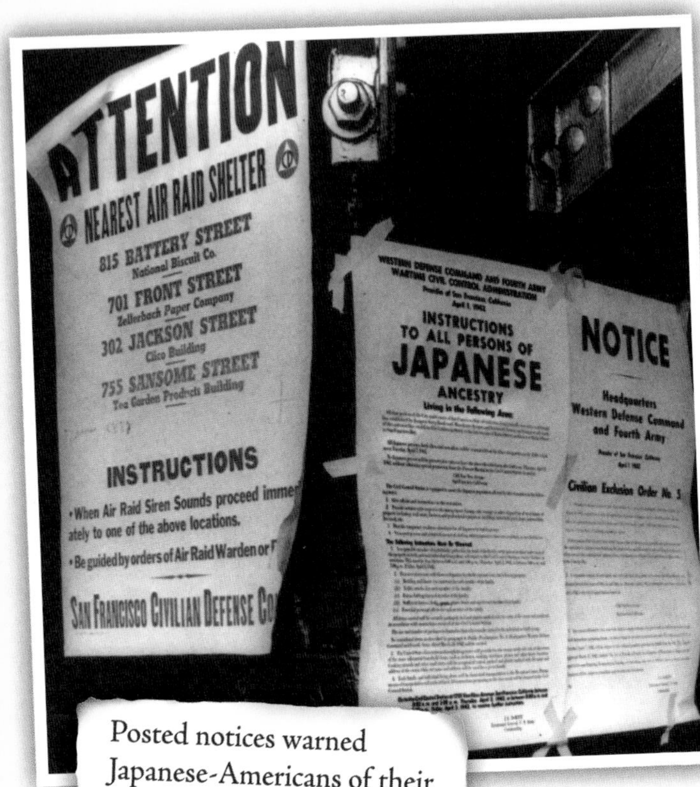

Posted notices warned Japanese-Americans of their pending evacuation.

Your father is deep in thought. "This isn't Germany," he finally says. "I know in my heart that our government will treat the Japanese-Americans much better than the Jews are being treated in Germany."

You still feel terrible for Toki and his family.

"In times of war," says your father, "people get carried away by fear. That makes them do things that are wrong. I want you to think about that."

You do think about it. You hate the Japanese who bombed Pearl Harbor, but you don't think Toki or any innocent person should be punished for it. You're afraid it will take Americans a long time to face up to that truth.

To follow another path, turn to page 229.
To read the conclusion, turn to page 321.

Your classmates want to know if you're going to destroy something from Japan. And suddenly a thought pops into your mind.

"No, I have a better plan to prove my loyalty," you say.

You remember hearing that your Scout troop was going to have a scrap metal drive. Your metal cars, trucks, trains, and other toys could be melted down to make weapons and equipment for the war.

At the next Boy Scout meeting, you ask your scout leader about the scrap metal drive. Mr. Landon explains that it's starting next week. He also says the Scouts will be searching for old tires and other rubber goods that can be turned into tank treads and tires for jeeps. You will also be looking for newspapers and other kinds of paper. It can be recycled to make material for packages sent overseas.

Bicycle tires and other rubber items were recycled.

As months go by, you read the paper and listen to the radio for news about the war. The more you learn, the more you want to help. One day your mom puts a thought into your mind.

Turn the page.

BUY WAR BONDS

"I'll tell you what," she says. "We'll pay you to do chores around the house. Once you get enough money, you can fill up your Victory Book."

You received your Victory Book weeks ago. You need to fill it up with stamps, which cost a dime each. Once you've placed 187 stamps in it, plus pay 5 cents, you can buy a war bond worth $18.75. The money goes to the war effort. In 10 years you can cash in the war bond for $25.

You've come a long way since the war began. You realize that Toki and his parents are good Americans even if they are of Japanese ancestry. And you know now that putting your toys and time to good use is far more helpful than destroying something made in Japan.

To follow another path, turn to page 229.
To read the conclusion, turn to page 321.

You're lucky your parents aren't home. You run to the dining room and gather plates, cups, and saucers and place them in a box. Soon you're racing through the woods. You find your friends in a small clearing.

"So you decided to show up," says Tommy. "Maybe you can prove your loyalty and we can still be friends."

"Of course," you reply. "I want to still be friends. I hate the Japanese we're fighting in the war. But I like Toki. What did Toki have to do with the bombing of Pearl Harbor?"

Your friends don't have an answer for you.

You dump the Japanese-made dishes on the ground. Tommy says that each of you will take turns smashing the dishes into little pieces. He says that you can go first.

You begin smashing away at the china. But it doesn't make you feel good or loyal. And now you are really mad at your friends.

"This is stupid!" you yell at Tommy. "My mom is going to have a fit! And how does this help us win the war?"

"Just go home, you traitor!" he screams.

"I'll go home," you reply. "But we're not friends anymore."

As you walk home to tell your mother what happened, you realize you don't even want to be friends with Tommy. You realize Toki is a much better friend.

To follow another path, turn to page 229.
To read the conclusion, turn to page 321.

TWICE A PATRIOT

EX-PRIVATE OBIE BARTLETT LOST LEFT ARM—PEARL HARBOR
RELEASED: DEC., 1941—NOW AT WORK WELDING
IN A WEST COAST SHIPYARD...

"Sometimes I feel my job here is as important as the one I had to leave

FIGHTING TWO WARS

You would like to shake hands with your 22-year-old son Albert, but you can't. You have no right arm.

It's March 1943. Albert is greeting you at the bus station in your hometown of Mobile, Alabama. You haven't seen him since you left to fight the war more than a year earlier. Your 24th Infantry Regiment was one of the first regiments to ship out. The American military is still segregated—blacks cannot fight alongside whites. So although trained in combat, you and other African-Americans were often placed in service roles instead.

Turn the page.

But bullets couldn't tell the difference between black and white, soldier and worker. Three weeks ago, on an island near Australia, a stray bullet shattered your arm. It had to be amputated. Now here you are, back home and out of the Army.

Although you are proud of your service overseas, you're looking forward to your new life. You saw enough of the horrors of war.

You hope the war has helped bring about changes in Alabama. Ever since birth you and others like you have been discriminated against in every walk of life.

You quickly find out nothing has changed. You risked your life for your country, but your country treats you as an inferior person. You know that African-Americans are mistreated in the North as well, but they can at least go to the same public places as whites.

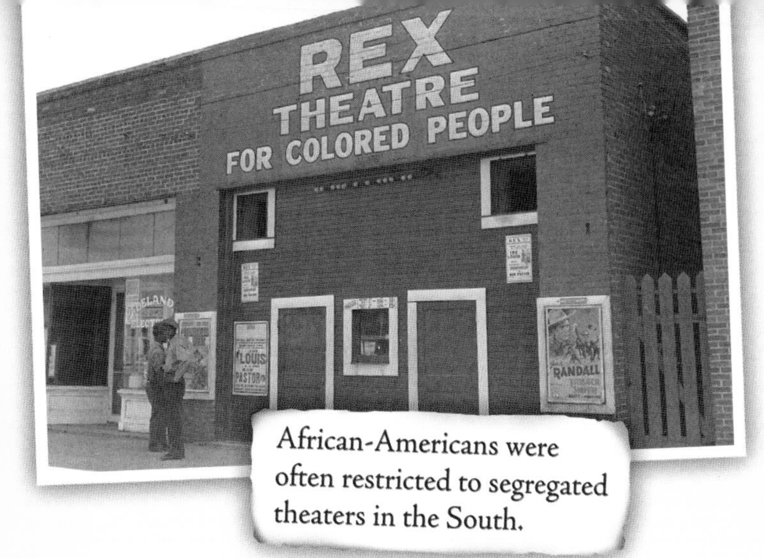

African-Americans were often restricted to segregated theaters in the South.

You recall an invitation from your old friend Sam to live with him and his family on his Illinois farm.

You are sick of Alabama. You will never forget what happened five years ago when your wife became ill. She died because a nearby hospital served only white patients and refused to admit her. By the time she arrived at the hospital for blacks, she was dead. But still, you have friends and relatives here. Do you take your family and move?

To move to Illinois, turn to page **294**.

To stay in Alabama, turn to page **296**.

You send a telegram to your friend Sam stating that you are coming to live with him. You begin packing your truck.

"What are you doing?" your younger son, Jack, asks.

"We're moving to Illinois," you reply. "I will not live as a second-class citizen anymore. We're fighting for freedom in Europe and Asia, and we have no freedom here in Alabama. Go tell Albert we're leaving."

Albert races into the room.

"Good!" he says. "I'm glad we're going. I can't get out of Alabama fast enough."

You are soon on your way to Illinois. When you arrive, Sam and his wife, Mary, take you and your sons to a nearby restaurant. You eat in the same room as whites for the first time in your life. It gives you a good feeling.

That good feeling disappears quickly when 18-year-old Jack opens his mouth.

"Dad, I want to serve in the Army, just like you did," he says. "They need me over there."

You know that is true. The Germans control almost all of Europe, and the Japanese are fierce fighters.

You also know that Jack could be killed. Why should he die for a country that treats African-Americans so badly? But you are proud of his courage.

To encourage Jack to volunteer, turn to page **298**.

To try to stop Jack from volunteering, turn to page **303**.

You enjoy getting a haircut because it allows you to sit quietly and think. So the week after you return home, you stop by the barbershop.

As you watch bits of your hair falling to the floor, you ponder whether to leave Alabama or join your friend on his farm in Illinois. You ask your barber, Joe, for his opinion.

"You have every good reason to leave," he says. "Our people are treated better up North than they are here. But I think you should stay. You owe something to the people of Mobile to help change things. Wouldn't it be great if someday Negroes could vote or go to the park with whites or attend the same schools? Maybe you can help make that happen."

You agree. By the time he is done clipping your hair, you have decided to stay.

A few weeks later, a letter from the draft board arrives. It's addressed to Albert. You know what it is before he opens it. Albert has been drafted.

An angry look appears on Albert's face as he reads the letter. He slams it on the table.

"I'm not fighting in any war for the United States," he says. "I went to an inferior school because I'm black. I can't vote because I'm black. In the eyes of Alabama, I'm not even good enough to swim in the same pool or sit in the same restaurant as a white person. Why should I help a country that won't help me?""

"You have no choice," you say. "You've been drafted. You have to go."

"We'll see about that," he says.

To let Albert make his own decision, turn to page **314**.

To convince him to report, turn to page **315**.

You look Jack straight in the eye and point to your right shoulder.

"Do you see this shoulder?" you ask him. "It means good luck to me."

"Good luck?" Jack answers with a puzzled look on his face. "How can it be good luck? There is no arm attached to that shoulder."

"There could have been no body attached to it," you respond. "I could have been killed. I was very lucky. But you might not be so lucky if you go off to fight. Is it worth risking your life for a country that thinks we are inferior to whites?"

"Yes, it is," Jack says. "I heard stories that the Germans are killing Jewish people all over Europe. They are murdering people in the countries they take over. We must defeat them."

"That's all I wanted to hear," you say. "I'm proud of you for standing up for what is right. Maybe if we risk our lives and do what's right overseas, then someday soon the leaders of this nation will do what's right for us right here in the United States."

Two days later Jack is gone. A few weeks later you receive a letter from him. He's training with the mostly African-American 92nd Infantry Division. You know he'll see combat in Europe.

Now it's Albert who has a question. He doesn't like farm life. He learned that factories making jeeps for the war are seeking workers in Detroit, Michigan. He wants to move there. You worry he could get into trouble living in Detroit on his own.

To move with Albert to Detroit, turn to page **300**.

To stay on the farm, turn to page **309**.

Sam is in the barn milking a cow.

"Sam, it was so nice of you to invite my family to live with you. But Albert and I are moving to Detroit. They need factory workers there. I'm sorry to leave."

A few days later you're driving to Detroit. It's early June 1943 and you are feeling good. But after one week on his factory job, Albert tells you something that turns your mood from joy to anger.

"I was talking with one of the white guys at the factory who started on the job last week," he says. "He told me he's going to get promoted long before I do. And even worse, I'm going to be put in a more dangerous job than he is. When I asked him why, he told me it was because I was a Negro."

You're mad, but not shocked. You know that African-Americans aren't just mistreated in the South. It happens nearly everywhere.

Blacks and whites worked together in wartime factories.

You realized that several days earlier when you were looking for an apartment. Some signs in front of the buildings read "No Negroes Allowed." You finally find an apartment that houses blacks in a section of town called Paradise Valley. It's not nearly as nice as the ones in which white people are living.

Turn the page.

Albert is upset about the discrimination you are dealing with. He hopes joining his new friends for some fun at the Belle Isle amusement park will take his mind off his troubles.

You're at home that night listening to music on the radio. Suddenly a news report interrupts the broadcast. Fighting has broken out between black teenagers and white sailors and teens. It began at the amusement park and spilled out into the city. You are worried.

To look for Albert, turn to page **306**.

To wait for him, turn to page **312**.

A restaurant is no place to talk to Jack about making the biggest decision of his young life. You wait until you get to your new home on your friend's farm. Then you speak to Jack at the kitchen table. "Why did we leave Alabama?" you ask. You already know the answer.

"Because of segregation," he answers. "A Negro can't reach his potential in Alabama."

"Has the United States government done anything to help Negroes in the South?" you ask.

Jack ponders the question. "I guess not," he says.

"When I got back home, I thought I would be treated with respect. But I was wrong. Our leaders have done nothing for us in the South. And we're treated badly in other parts of the country too. I don't want you helping this country until it shows it can help us."

Turn the page.

Your words make sense to you, but not to Jack. He has not changed his mind.

"I still want to join the Army just like you did," he says.

Jack says nothing for two days. You start hoping that you have convinced him to stay on the farm. But one morning he is not at the breakfast table. You knock on his door to wake him up, but there is no answer. You peek inside. The bed is made and he is gone. There's a note on a nearby chair. It reads:

Dear Dad and Albert:

By the time you read this, I will be on a bus to New York. I am off to join the war. I will make you both proud.

Love, Jack

African-American soldiers stand at attention during an army inspection.

You are angry that Jack went against your wishes. But you can't help but be proud of him too. You just hope and pray he will return home alive.

THE END

To follow another path, turn to page 229.
To read the conclusion, turn to page 321.

Visions of Albert being hurt race through your mind. You can't sit and do nothing. Soon you're driving downtown. You see police cars everywhere. You can't drive through, so you park and approach one of the police officers.

"Just go home!" the officer says. "Can't you see that we have a riot on our hands here?"

You are about to leave when you notice Albert. He looks confused and scared. He has blood all over his face and hands.

"That's my son, that's my son!" you tell the officer. "I must get him out of here! Albert! Albert!"

He sees you and runs as fast as he can to you. You grab his bloody hand and race toward the car. You hear gunshots and pray one doesn't find you or your son. You finally feel safe when you reach the car and start driving home.

Police fired tear gas as white rioters fled a black neighborhood in Detroit.

Soon Albert is telling you all about the riot. "When we got to the amusement park," he says, "some white teenagers and sailors were beating up some of our friends. We had to defend our buddies, so we joined the fight. Before you knew it, more guys got involved and there was a big battle."

Turn the page.

"Pretty soon it was a riot," he continues. "The fighting spilled over into the city. Negroes were attacking any white people they saw. And whites were attacking innocent Negroes. It was horrible."

"What were you doing?" you ask.

"By that time I was just watching. I wanted to get out of there. But the police couldn't control what was going on. Three white guys attacked me. That's how I got all bloody. Then the police starting shooting. I lay there so I wouldn't get hit by bullets. When the shooting was over, there were a bunch of people dead on the ground. But stop worrying. I'm all right now."

"You're going to stay all right," you reply. "We're leaving Detroit and going back to Sam's farm. At least there we can find some peace."

THE END

To follow another path, turn to page 229.
To read the conclusion, turn to page 321.

You remember listening to President Roosevelt on the radio. He often said that every American must do his or her part to win the war.

You tried to do your part in the Army. But even though you lost your right arm, you feel there is more you can do. You decide to stay on Sam's farm and help grow food for the war effort.

Albert is big and strong and finds the farm work difficult but satisfying. He has even talked about owning his own farm someday. You'd like to help more, but you can't do heavy labor. So you decide you can help Sam make the most out of his farm.

You head to Alabama to talk to a farmer named Buck you met years ago. Buck had learned farming techniques in the early 1930s from a Tuskegee Institute graduate. The man trained years earlier under the great African-American scientist George Washington Carver.

Turn the page.

You spend two weeks learning everything you can about farming from Buck. He shows you the best way to treat the soil, rotate and water the crops, and the best crops to grow in various climates.

You return to Illinois and show Sam everything Buck taught you. Sam is impressed. He sits at his kitchen table and studies the information. With you and Albert helping, he treats the soil in his fields just as Buck explained.

"Look at my crops," Sam says several months later. "They are growing bigger and better than they ever have. And I have you and Buck to thank for it. The soldiers who eat these vegetables won't go away hungry. Maybe your son Jack will end up eating one of these carrots!"

You feel as if you have indeed done your job to help the war effort. You can't do too much work on the farm with one arm. But as President Roosevelt said, you do what you can. And you feel proud.

To follow another path, turn to page 229.
To read the conclusion, turn to page 321.

You are frozen with fear. You think about driving downtown to try to find Albert. But you don't think you can track him down.

Suddenly the phone rings. The noise and your fear combine to make you jump from your chair. You answer the phone. It's the police.

"We are sorry, but we have reason to believe that your son was killed in the riot tonight," says the voice on the other end. "We need you to come down to the morgue and identify the body."

You feel as if all the life has drained out of you. You can barely drag yourself to your car. You don't know if you can concentrate on driving two miles to the morgue. But even though you are in a daze, you make it safely. An attendant meets you at the door and takes you to a back room. A body with a sheet over it awaits you. The sheet is pulled back.

"Is this your son?" you are asked.

It is Albert. There is a bullet hole in his neck. You say nothing. You just nod and walk away. You have never felt such grief.

Only one thought is going through your mind. You wish you had gone downtown to find Albert and get him away from the violence. If you had, perhaps he would still be alive. Maybe you would have been killed. But you would have gladly given your life to save Albert.

And now it is too late.

THE END

To follow another path, turn to page 229.
To read the conclusion, turn to page 321.

Albert's bags are packed. And soon he's gone. He told you he was reporting for the draft, and you hope it's true.

A week later you receive a letter in the mail. There is no return address. A feeling of shock and horror washes over you as you read it.

"I have sneaked out of training," Albert writes. "I will tell nobody where I am. I will not fight for this country. I am headed to Canada, where I can be treated more like a man than I can here."

Your mind is racing. You know if Albert gets caught, he's going to jail. And you know wherever he goes, he'll have to deal with hatred from some people.

Will you ever see him again? Tears start rolling down your cheeks. You can only hope that someday, you'll be reunited.

THE END

To follow another path, turn to page 229.
To read the conclusion, turn to page 321.

African-Americans were allowed to enlist in the Army Air Corps for the first time in 1941.

You walk slowly to the door and stand in front of it. You hold up the only arm you have.

"I will not let you leave this house," you tell Albert sternly. "You are going to report to basic training and you will fight overseas. Your country needs you."

"How do they need me?" Albert asks.

Turn the page.

"The Germans are not just treating Jews and others badly like Negroes are being treated here," you say. "They are killing millions of people. They are trying to take over the world. They must be stopped. You would be fighting to save the world."

You have made an impression on your son. You leave him alone to think. Five minutes later, he visits you in the kitchen.

"You're right," he says. "I never thought about it that way. I will report."

You are proud when Albert volunteers to be trained as a Tuskegee Airman. You are even more proud when he performs so well that he is sent overseas to fly a P-51 Mustang fighter plane.

He writes how he and his fellow pilots painted the tails on their planes bright red. That way the American bombers they were escorting, as well as the German pilots, would know who they were.

Pilots posed on an airplane at the Tuskegee Army Airfield during World War II.

Many months pass. On a cold morning in February 1945, you notice two soldiers walking toward your house. One is carrying a telegram. Before they even reach your door, you know the bad news they're bringing. Albert has been killed in action.

Turn the page.

"Your son has died a hero," says one soldier. "He was shot down on a mission over Germany. Your son was a fine pilot. You should be proud."

You are proud. But as you sit on the couch and cry, you wonder if you did the right thing by talking Albert into fighting the war.

You know that Albert wasn't alone. Thousands of American troops have been killed. You realize that Albert was doing his duty. As he said, he was trying to help save the world.

You know that you will shed more tears as time goes by. But you also know that the soldier was right: Albert indeed died a hero.

To follow another path, turn to page 229.
To read the conclusion, turn to page 321.

The Tuskegee Airmen flew more than 15,000 missions in Africa, Italy, and Germany.

About 3 million women worked in military factories during the war.

CHAPTER 5

A NEW WORLD

World War II changed life for everyone—those who fought and those who stayed on the home front.

Most women returned to their lives as housewives after the war. But those who helped the war effort by taking jobs felt a sense of pride and satisfaction. Their efforts planted the seeds of the women's movement a generation later. By the early 1970s, women were forging careers all over the United States.

A Japanese-American child awaited evacuation in California.

After the war Japanese Americans slowly rebuilt their lives. In 1976, the 200th anniversary of the founding of the country, the president of the United States admitted mistakes were made on the home front during World War II.

President Gerald Ford said, "We now know what we should have known then—not only was that evacuation wrong, but Japanese-Americans were and are loyal Americans."

The contributions made by black soldiers in World War II forever changed their position in the United States. Soon after the war, the armed services integrated. No longer were blacks separated from whites. They would fight side-by-side in future wars. Soon blacks began demanding and winning equality in all walks of American life.

Americans gained confidence through their efforts as soldiers and on the home front during World War II. They felt great pride at helping return peace and freedom to the people of Europe and Asia. And as President Roosevelt asked, everyone seemed to do his or her part.

Timeline

1939—World War II begins as Germany invades Poland September 1.

France and Great Britain declare war on Germany two days later.

1940—President Franklin D. Roosevelt asks Congress for more money for military spending in May.

France surrenders to Germany in June.

Congress enacts the first peacetime draft in American history

1941—The Lend-Lease program, in which the United States provides war material for countries fighting Germany, is signed into law.

Tuskegee Institute in Tuskegee, Alabama, begins training black pilots.

Japanese warplanes bomb Pearl Harbor December 7; the U.S. declares war on Japan the next day.

Japan, Italy and Germany declare war on the United States.

1942—An order signed by President Roosevelt declares that all Americans of Japanese descent living in the western U.S. must be relocated.

Rationing of such items as coffee and gasoline begins.

1943—Race riots strike Detroit in June.

1944—One June 6 Allied forces land in France as the D-Day invasion begins.

France is liberated from German rule as Allied forces march into Paris in August.

German troops launch the Battle of the Bulge in Belgium in December.

1945—Franklin Roosevelt dies April 12 and is succeeded as president by Harry Truman.

German dictator Adolf Hitler commits suicide April 30; Germany surrenders May 7.

An atomic bomb is dropped on the Japanese city of Hiroshima August 6; another atomic bomb is dropped on the Japanese city of Nagasaki three days later.

Japan formally surrenders September 2, ending the war.

Other Paths to Explore

In this book you've seen how the events experienced during World War II look different from three points of view.

Perspectives on history are as varied as the people who lived it. You can explore other paths on your own to learn more about what happened. Seeing history from many points of view is an important part of understanding it.

Here are ideas for other World War II points of view to explore:

- Japanese-Americans weren't the only people not trusted during World War II. What would it have been like to be of German or Italian descent in the United States during wartime?
- Some men who wanted to fight in the war were classified as "4-F." That meant they were physically unable to go into battle. What would it have been like not being able to serve?
- The most noted canteens during World War II featured movie stars and other famous people entertaining American troops. What would it have been like to spend time at such places?